Not the Usual Suspects

Beyond the Batterer: Abusive Power in Politics

Pamela Jayne

Michigan ✦ PowerDogPress

Published by PowerDogPress

PowerDogPress, Michigan

ISBN: 978-0-9993005-1-0

Table of Contents

Acknowledgments

This book is dedicated to powerful people who decide that their power should never be misused for merely selfish aims. I include political leaders of all stripes in this group, some of whom consistently use their power to promote the overall good. Thank you.

The book is also dedicated to people who have been subjected to abusive ideas and actions and feel powerless as a result. I hope they find something here worthy of possibility and hope.

Finally, I dedicate this book to all of the people who have given their valuable time in the effort to stop abusive behavior and help victims heal. Those jobs are difficult ones, yet they do them with persistence and integrity, and without hesitation.

Thanks to my editor, GillianRyan Publishing, and to all of my friends, co-workers and family who read and reviewed this book and patiently listened to me talk about it for way too long.

Author's Note

If we want to understand how batterers operate—how they intimidate and bully and frighten people—then we need only consider Donald Trump as a case study. Trump is the epitome, in every way, of abusiveness; he is no different than many of the men with whom I have worked over the years in domestic violence counseling groups. In my book, *Ditch that Jerk*, I let people in on what abusers really think and then classify them into categories based on their likelihood of change: the good, the bad and the hopeless. Trump is, in my view, hopeless—unlikely to ever change, unless he is constrained by outside forces. That's an obvious problem.

But this is not a book about Donald Trump. In fact, the vast majority of it was written in 2000, long before his arrival onto the political scene. That's because Trump, albeit abusive, is not the cause of abusive political culture. He is just its personification. When he is gone, as he will certainly be, the abusive political culture will go merrily on without him—the problem didn't begin, nor will it end, with him. We shouldn't be lulled into thinking that once he has been vanquished our problems will be over, because whether he is a symptom or the actual disease, he is clearly contagious and others like him, or worse, are on the horizon.

As I claim throughout, we can learn about abusive politics from examining the characteristics and effects of the domestic abuser and we can learn about the domestic abuser from focusing on abusive political culture. And learn we must. A little knowledge might be a dangerous thing, but a total lack of it is very much worse.

I have used only a few examples of political abusiveness because there are so many that I couldn't expose even a tiny fraction of them. The book is more about general ideas to which daily behaviors can be usefully applied. We should ask ourselves where and in whom we've seen these tactics, motives and beliefs before—and what the result was.

Want to weigh in? Want to add your own examples? Send an email to pamelajayne@powerdogpress.com and stay tuned for new ways to connect.

Chapter 1

Just the Way Things Are

Hate and force cannot be in just a part of the world
without having an effect on the rest of it.

—Eleanor Roosevelt

For over a decade, I worked with domestic abusers—people who commit the crime of domestic violence. In that time, as my clients revealed to me their motivations, I gradually came to understand the connections between how they see the world and the abuse and violence that result. I was privileged to witness first-hand the processes that have led them to and, in some cases, away from a life of violence and abuse. The composite story they tell is that their behavior should come as no surprise. After all, it didn't show up out of nowhere; rather, their abusive behavior was the predictable result of their everyday thoughts, feelings and desires. Their abuse is the tangible expression of how they view and understand the world.

In this book, we will hear directly from domestic abusers. They will show us what abuse looks like—it's not as clear-cut as you might think—what motivates them to use it, and what it's like to contemplate change. But that's just the first step in our effort here. In order to truly understand why violence persists despite unprecedented access to resources

1

and professional expertise, we have to look far beyond those who get arrested and labeled for it.

Violence and abuse do not exist because of some character deficit in a few men who get caught and branded as domestic abusers—they're just the usual suspects. Violence exists because we live in a culture in which violence and abuse are celebrated and reinforced, and within which an abundance of abusive behavior, coming from the highest of places, is carefully watched, applauded and very widely modeled.

Domestic violence counselors know that abusers hold an identifiable worldview—a belief system that is more or less common amongst them. We know what it looks like, a little something about what motivates it and we know to where it leads. Unfortunately, another variant of that worldview has been showing up elsewhere—not in the homes of domestic abusers but out in the world, among those not usually suspected of anything at all.

I hope to show that what ordinary domestic abusers and their more prominent counterparts *say* is more than just the inconsequential ramblings of a few crazy people. It is, in fact, part of a consistent and coherent worldview with very wide effects. To that end, I will introduce the actions, motives and beliefs embraced by the usual domestic abuser and encourage us to ask ourselves a very important question: *Where have we seen this kind of behavior before?*

The point is a simple, if controversial one. Domestic abusers, about whom I know quite a bit, hold beliefs that promote and allow for abusive behavior. Their tactics are all in pursuit of getting more power; the consequences they produce are dire. But other, more powerful people—our purported influencers and leaders—use similar tactics and produce similarly awful and widespread consequences.

Before I get further into it, let's get a few points in order. First, I will use the term violence and abuse interchangeably, but we should remember that violence is just one expression of the abuser's mindset. Most abusers use violence rarely, if at all, and yet they control, coerce and devastate their victims just as if their abuse came in a physically violent form.

Second, most people are not abusers. They don't abuse their families and they don't act abusively from their positions of power. It's important to keep that in mind lest we start to believe that everybody is abusive, or that it's *just the way things are*. Abusers want us to think that their behaviors are common and everyday—*just the way things are*—because that gives them a convenient excuse and justification for keeping it up.

You may be wondering who I am referring to when I use the term "unusual suspect." Who are the kinds of people I believe to be abusive on a larger scale and where do we find them? Of course, they can be anyone and they can be prominent in many places such as media, politics and business, but what they have in common, for our purposes anyhow, is that they either hold positions of power or they want to. Therefore, we need to be able to identify them quickly and pick them out from among their peers.

Since none of them wear hats proclaiming their intent to behave abusively, with some notable recent exceptions, we need a reliable way to tell who's who. Fortunately, there are some obvious signs—and some subtle ones, too—that will help us sort them out. We'll get to that. For now, let's focus on the most important of our questions: *So what? What does it matter if a few leaders and other influential personalities use abusive tactics and think in abusive ways? They are all like that, aren't they? How bad can it be?*

From decades of direct work with abusers, I can say without qualification that abusive people create considerable damage—many are very good at their job of abusing people and seeking power. It's important to know which beliefs they hold because they—especially our leaders—will absolutely act on them eventually. The more unfettered their power, so much the worse for all of us. One person can make quite a mess of things.

I have known many hundreds of domestic abusers over the course of my career and I can state with confidence that *how people are* always shows up in *what they do*. And people who hold abusive beliefs always produce negative effects in ways big and small—in their homes and out in the world. Always. When these people are also high-profile, they have an awful lot of power to use for good or ill. They are given a forum within which they can influence national and even world events, so we'd better know as much as possible about them. After all, do we really want people with an abusive mentality to be making decisions about what happens to us?

Even more importantly, powerful, high-visibility people are models who give others permission and encouragement to follow their example. They provide their audiences with a solid reason to adopt and express obviously abusive ideas. Therefore, we ought to make sure that our models are the right ones. We need to know who these people are, how they think, and what they want in order to predict what they'll do or prevent them from gaining further power. Acting out an abusive mentality is quite profitable, after all, and only when it isn't and the costs of embracing it exceed the costs of changing it, will anything be any different.

I know that some people will say, "Wait a minute! Are you saying that our political leadership and other assorted people of power and influence are abusers? Are you claiming that they are violent? What are you talking about?"

It's true that some of these people *are* violent—we have seen it first-hand—but that's not the main point. I am arguing that there is a worldview—a mentality—that allows for and condones abusive behavior and that people we would never think to label as abusers subscribe to and act out that view on a regular basis. They may not be physically violent, but their beliefs and the actions that flow from them cause harm and are, by most any definition, abusive in both intent and consequence. That's why we have to pay close attention to them. They may be hard to recognize; they may not be the "usual suspects"—a name reserved for the everyday domestic abuser—but they, too, can cause damage before we figure out what they're up to.

I will surely be asked whether this is a partisan piece of work. Is it just a right-wing-bashing book? It's true that the traits, motives and actions described here are most often associated with a right-wing outlook. But labels don't seem to mean much anymore; there is no longer a litmus test to determine who belongs at which end of the political spectrum, and so membership in this club is not exclusive. Sadly, it's wide open and it will be up to you to decide who fits the bill.

I want to clarify who the actual subjects of this book are, as there are lots of possibilities—there is plenty of abuse to go around! We can't cover everyone, so we'll focus primarily on those for whom exposure is key. In other words, there is obvious abusive behavior out there in the world that barely needs mention—we all understand that it's abusive; pointing it out would be like shooting fish in a barrel. Where's the challenge? Instead, we'll focus on the influential purveyors of abusive worldviews whose takes are much more subversive, stealthy and beguiling. Some of these abusers tell us that their views and the actions that flow from them are the morally right ones, even as they cause harm.

So, how can we tell the difference between the two? With the first group—the obvious abusers—we can easily argue that the abusive worldview is present. In games and movies and some kinds of music, violence is glorified and misogyny is standard fare. In these sources, violence and misogyny are so explicitly stated that it's not a big stretch to conclude those artists are not good role models for alleviating violence. The music's message is direct, blatant and obvious. But here is the thing: Their proponents and creators don't tell us that their music is actually good for us or, in some sense, moral and right. In other words, they don't disguise their music and message under a cloak of *supposed* morality. They know what they are saying and even if we don't like it, at least we won't be fooled into believing that it represents something that it doesn't.

But the second group—the ones who are more subversive—disguise their abuse as morally "right." For example, some of the family values crowd may say that beating kids and demanding total obedience will make those kids stronger people, but we know that that kind of treatment only creates people who are aggressive and angry. We may be told by any number of abusive worldview-ers that people who are poor are so because they deserve it, or that "right living" people shouldn't have to pay the health care costs for people who may have eaten too much cake and otherwise behaved irresponsibly, or that selfish resource grabbing is actually the right, natural and even moral way to be. It's important to unmask these views and reveal the actual effects that they produce. Our purpose here is to understand and expose specific groups that promote and carry the abusive worldview—people we may have never before considered.

Who is this book for?

Those of us who witness but do not share the abusive culture are nonetheless subjected to it. We can't get away. Only those who never watch TV or listen to the radio or read books or magazines or newspapers or go online or even go outside can escape being touched—tainted—by this ideology. But if you are the target of attacks by those with an abusive mindset, that is, if you are gay or liberal or a woman; if you are a from another country, or a different religion or even no religion; if you are a minority; if you are not rich, this book may help explain why you feel so frustrated, confused and powerless in today's American culture. Of course you feel that way! It's practically by design.

These are natural feelings for anyone involved with the promoters of abusive ideas and anyone who is subject to their tactics. Whether it is abuse in your home or from powerful men and women in the public eye—such as media, Congress, or the Oval Office—please know that you aren't crazy. You aren't hysterical or overreacting. Anger and upset are warning signs that something may be wrong—that something has gone awry. Well, something *is* wrong and something *has* gone awry.

Nonetheless, many of us have been warned to let bygones be bygones in the face of the expansion of this abusive mentality. "Just forget about it," we are told. Let me assure you that this is a common refrain of abusive people. Saying that something is political, for example, and therefore out of bounds for polite talk, is just a tactic to get us to be quiet and to keep us from calling out bad behavior. No matter how they get us to stop talking about abusive behavior, however they silence us, it's a problem because abusive people who are allowed to *just forget about it* and are not held accountable for their actions, are much more likely to repeat them.

Not the Usual Suspects

Yale Professor Tim Snyder writes, in his book *On Tyranny*, that when abusive, power-mongering forces come to call, there is a small window of opportunity to resist. If those forces get away with their behavior for very long, resistance, as the saying goes, becomes futile. To accept abusive power-mongering as normal or inevitable—as *just the way things are*—is to give permission for its spread.[1]

TV talk show host Tucker Carlson once said to those voicing concern over some aspect of the political situation, "You guys really believe that politics can change people's lives."[2] He wanted us to stop taking it all so seriously. He acted like it was just a game. And maybe for some that's true. But what Carlson failed to appreciate is that politics is about power relations among people and, therefore, can and does change people's lives. Ask the victims of the holocaust; ask the people in Sudan, Rwanda, Syria, Iraq, and the French and American revolutions. Ask them whether politics changes anybody's life. Politics, after all, is about who has power and what they do with it.

Domestic violence, regardless of what else we might say about it, is about exactly the same sort of power relationship—it's politics in action. Who has the power and what do they do with it? And those politics—those power relationships— change people's lives for better and for worse. If they can create shame in us for being political and silence us, the exposure that they dread becomes less likely.

If you are a professional in domestic violence, whether you work with victims or with abusers, this book is a good reminder of what we already know: Violence in people's homes and out in the world is connected and consequential. We aren't going to get rid of domestic violence by holding a few abusers' groups, building a few shelters or changing a few laws. The problem is a lot bigger than that. However, sometimes that point is very hard to make. Many people think that alcohol, lack of communication and mental illness are the problems, and it's hard to convince them otherwise. This book provides an opportunity to view the source of violence and abuse from a different perspective. It's a chance to see that abuse isn't about a mental illness and doesn't come from a fifth of vodka, but that it arises out of a whole, widely shared view of the world in which behaving abusively is an obvious and acceptable option used by the most politically powerful among us.

But that is not the whole of it. We must ask what these connections mean, what they foretell, and what professionals in the field of domestic violence ought to do about it. I don't mean just within our own work arenas and with our own clients, but out in our communities where we strive to educate, break the cycle and effect change.

Unfortunately, we will never be able to effectively or helpfully deal with the abuser so long as he can see quite plainly that his behavior is not deviant but mainstream and, worse, downright profitable. Instead of limiting the opportunities for the abusive mentality to expand, we are making a new place for it.

Just as an abuser renders a home, a place of supposed security, so unsafe that people cannot live there, one day, it is possible that none of us will be safe, either. When an abusive mindset is in charge, we are at risk. Exposing it, identifying those who carry it, and examining its consequences are job one. When we are finished, we will consider how we might resist, if not change it.

It can be therapeutic to know that you aren't alone; that many others feel the same, that's it's not your fault that things have turned out so badly, and that there are ways to fight back this encroaching abusiveness. I hope that some of the ideas presented here will work towards those therapeutic ends.

Finally, if you are one of the people who listens to and believes in this abusive mindset, I can only ask that you keep an open mind and ask yourself whether these people and what they're selling is ultimately anything you want to buy. I hope that you ask yourself whether these consequences are ones that are acceptable for us and for those who will follow you. Because what kind of world we want this to be is a legitimate and urgent question.

Armando's story

Armando, a participant in one of my abuse intervention groups, grew up in an abusive home. He spent his childhood anxious and afraid. He told his wife, "You are never going to beat me at anything. I've been through it all. You will never win."

What did he mean by that? He was telling her never to cross him. He was too formidable a foe; she was in no way equal to him. And after many months of witnessing just how true that statement was, she gave up trying to make things better. She could make no difference, no change. She no longer made many decisions for herself, let alone for her family. She basically spoke to nobody and when she did, she revealed little because she didn't know whether anyone could be trusted. She no longer contributed anything—she was incapacitated, a mere bystander to life; invisible. She didn't understand what happened or how she got to be that way. But Armando knew; her debilitation and dependence just made him feel stronger and more in control.

This example shows just how devastating abuse is for people. Abusive tactics like this one are every bit as destructive—maybe even more destructive—as actual physical violence. But these kinds of effects are not just limited to an abuser's home. As we will cover in subsequent chapters, the fallout from abusive behavior among our unusual suspects is a true disaster, too. People exposed to abusive culture often become complacent and apathetic. They don't engage with the world. They don't participate in civic life. They don't vote. They seem to not even care and why should they, after all? It too often feels that nothing they do makes any difference anyhow and they, like Armando's wife, just feel hopeless. I will argue in the last chapter that such conclusions, while understandable, are misguided. There is hope. There are things we can do to save ourselves. We still matter.

An unusual suspect profile: Bill O'Reilly

According to Bill O'Reilly, he grew up in an abusive home; he said that he feared his father might actually kill him. He tells us that his father's favorite refrain was, "Shut up," and that in his family, "there were never any timeouts but plenty of knockouts."[3]

Yet, he took to the TV stage night after night on his show, *The No Spin Zone*, and pummeled his guests: "Shut up! Shut up!" He would accuse his guests of lying and spinning, which was a violation of his on-air no lying policy—a policy from which he always exempted himself. The irony of his no-spin rule is that a more pronounced spin can hardly be imagined than O'Reilly turning the abusive treatment he suffered as a child into something interesting and fun—something that is just no problem at all.

O'Reilly's disturbing upbringing conspired with the abusive worldview to recreate, maintain and even celebrate the kind of abusiveness he once experienced. His abusive home became an abusive television show, but he's no longer the victim—he's the perpetrator; his abusiveness barely concealed under a veneer of total self-righteousness. He sold abuse and degradation and millions watched him do it. He modeled abuse and bullying and turned it into entertainment from which he profited greatly.

Was that inevitable? Did his upbringing make it impossible for him to become anything else? No, Bill still had choices.

For example, he could have dealt with his probably deep-seated feelings of powerlessness and fear—an option the abusive culture rarely allows—and decided never to subject anyone else to the kind of treatment he endured. Or he could do what he has done, which is project fear and anger and feelings of powerlessness out into the world, becoming that which he so detests and harming people in the process. He was bullied and put down—abused—so now he bullies and puts down and abuses others.

Sadly, we live within an abusive culture just waiting to welcome O'Reilly and plenty of others like him; a place of refuge, a home, and for some it seems, a veritable goldmine.

Chapter 2

How to Get More

Without reflection, we go blindly on our way,
creating more unintended consequences and
failing to achieve anything useful.

—Margaret J. Wheatley

A friend of mine who works in a counseling program for men convicted of domestic violence has always wanted to write a book for those men. I said to her, "Well, ya know, men don't read self-help books."

She said, "Oh, they'll wanna read this one."

"Why is that?" I asked.

"Because," she said, "I'm going to call it *How to Get More*."

I thought she was joking. "That's not what the book is about, though, right?"

She replied, "Well, yes it is."

"It *is?* Are you kidding?"

"Well," she explained, "I always tell them in my groups that if they start treating their partners better, they will probably also get more of what they *really* want."

I had to admit then that she was onto something important. Meet people where they are and communicate in their own language. Those are strategies that domestic violence professionals haven't always been very good at, frankly. We talk amongst ourselves and use a lot of jargon because esoteric language is one of the ways we remind ourselves that we are a real profession. We discuss privilege and entitlement, feminism and the social construction of masculinity as a matter of course, as if we all understand precisely what that means, which, of course, we do. But we forget that other people who have not been exposed to these ideas have no idea what we are talking about. And so we divide the world up into two factions: those who get it and those who don't.

The people we label as domestic abusers are not often receptive to our ideas. In other words, they rarely get it. Neither do most of the people in our communities, whom we seek to educate on the causes and effects of domestic violence and ways to prevent it. Ask any member of any well-meaning civic organization how it is that our socially constructed concept of, say, manhood leads to violence against women or how it is that a dominant group goes about rationalizing their derogation and oppression of minority groups and that well-meaning civic-minded citizen will look at you like you have three heads. "Violence, domestic violence," they might say, "That's caused by drinking, right?"

In professional antiviolence work, we confront the monumental task of convincing abusive people that the way in which they have been wielding their power is no good for anyone, including them, without actually saying so directly. We don't say straight out, for example, "Stop dominating. You'll be much happier if you don't try to control everybody and everything all the time." We don't say that because we know it would run headlong smack against all the other messages they get from everyplace else. It would just not work.

For example, it's rarely effective to say to a man in a domestic violence counseling group, "I know that rich, famous, important people who manage world affairs and make lots of money also behave in controlling, abusive and violent ways and probably have throughout history. I also know that those people are rewarded for their bad behavior most of the time, but just because they do it does not mean you have to." How credible are we when we imply that a man ought to be a little less powerful, a little softer, a better listener, maybe a tad less controlling and a little less...well, masculine? Although we don't say it quite that way, I'm sure that's what a great many of them hear: "Welcome to domestic violence class. For the next twenty-six weeks, we'll be teaching you how to become weak and powerless."

Clearly, we need to offer a message very different, more appealing, more motivational. So we do that as best we can. We reframe it. We strive to define power as something other than domination; independence as something other than closed-minded selfishness and isolation; perseverance as something other than obstinacy; and pride as something other than arrogant superiority, just for example. We search for illustrations of concepts like power and heroism and strength that really exemplify power and heroism and strength. But sadly, such examples aren't easy to find.

Noted linguist and author George Lakoff uses the term *hyper*-cognition in his writing to refer to those times when we just can't find the right word to make our point—no word exactly fits. That happens often enough, at least to me it does. But there is another term, which Lakoff also puts forth, to describe the circumstance where it's not just a word that we lack but an entire concept.[4]

That's called *hypo*-cognition and it fits the domestic violence field's dilemma precisely. We aren't missing a word; we are missing a concept. What do we want from batterers? Is it non-violence? Cooperation? What about peacefulness or 'non-controllingness'? What's the affirming and appealing concept that we seek? We don't exactly know. We have no word. How can we promote a positive alternative to abuse when we've never clearly identified one?

In 2016, one of the Oxford dictionary's notable words of the year was the Danish, *hygge*, defined as "a quality of coziness and comfortable conviviality that engenders a feeling of contentment and well being."[5] It's a nice word that efficiently captures something that could not otherwise be described without using a bunch of words. We don't have a word like that for our vision. What do we call a person who uses power for good and not to dominate or control? What is the opposite of abuse? What is that everyday word that describes what we mean and what we want?

Still, we try. I hear people speaking eloquently about domestic violence all the time. Some are absolutely brilliant, but they speak in an esoteric way that all but obscures their message. It doesn't matter how smart we are in our analysis of violence if nobody understands it. What good is it if nobody, save a few of us, actually *gets it*?

This problem is compounded by the increasingly stiff competition for ideas and it's hard to be heard these days. While we stumble and fumble around talking about non-violence, trying to get a better grasp of that elusive idea, the competition is talking about how to get, use and keep power without feeling much guilt over it. Our utopian visions, such as they are, like ending violence, while entirely laudable, are no match for the 'how to get it all for yourself and feel good about it' messages that are absolutely ubiquitous today. They talk about winning and getting more. In comparison, our conversation appears to be about losing and getting less. Which sounds more appealing?

Unless we can identify the concept along with a word that describes it and then learn to communicate it in a clear, resonant and widely compelling way, our persuasive abilities will remain limited. We, ourselves, have to know what it is before we can explain to others why they should want it, especially those who would be just as happy never to hear from us at all. The parallel to today's political environment is obvious. Progressives are baffled about why their messages seem to have fallen flat. How could so many people have accepted a worldview so chock full of clearly abusive ideas? What's wrong with them?

People always ask domestic violence professionals why the victim stays and puts up with abusive behavior. Why doesn't she just leave? With those questions, people are asking whether it's her fault for putting up with it or for being naïve in believing the abuser's lies and apologies. *How could she fall for such obvious drivel*, some people wonder. *What's wrong with her?* And we ask ourselves the same questions about the support that so many people give our political and cultural leaders. *What's wrong with those people who believed in these abusive leaders and would-be leaders who are so harmful to their interests?* We wonder, *don't they realize that they are being taken for a ride?*

Another way in which this question has been asked, for example, by journalist Thomas Frank in his best-selling book by the same name, is as follows: *What's the Matter with Kansas?*[6] In other words, why do people in Middle America vote for the people and the party that is so antithetical to their interests? What in the world is the matter with them? But that question is the wrong one and just as wrong as the question as to why victims stay with people who abuse them. The question isn't *What's wrong with them that they buy into this abusive mindset?* but *How does the leadership manage to disguise its real motives so well?* The question isn't *Why do those people believe?* but *How do those pundits and politicians manage to sound so convincing?*

Abusive men hook their partners in with romance and flattery and praise. They put their girlfriends and wives on a pedestal and promise a perfect union and a perfect life— *it's you and me baby against the world!* People buy into the abuser's picture of the world. But the rubber always meets the road eventually and people wind up with something altogether different than what was promised.

For lots of victims, by the time the *reality* sets in and she realizes that this relationship isn't what she signed up for, it's awfully hard—for all kinds of reasons—to get out. Hopefully we won't have to wait until the reality of the abusive mindset becomes devastatingly obvious. We need to be paying attention. We need a warning system and an action plan.

If we are ever going to see a marked reduction in violence, we will have to come to grips with what we as a culture are doing to create it and maintain it. In some ways, which we mostly don't see, we give permission and even encouragement to people who are abusive. If any meaningful change in our world is to occur, if violence is ever to be lessened in any real way, we will need to end our standard practice of compartmentalizing it, of seeing violence as the bad thing that a few bad people do. We will need to give up the hope that if we throw a few folks in jail or give them big fines or dress them up in orange jumpsuits and make them clean up garbage by the side of the road that we will have done enough, that we will have done something at all—that we are, at the very least, containing the problem. To really confront "the problem," we must look way beyond the usual suspects.

As professionals working to help end violence, we teach—or try to—about a way of life that clashes sharply with what abusers see all around them. We expose the beliefs, values and thought processes that lead to violence and encourage them to look for alternatives. We begin a conversation about the futility of control, abuse and violence, meanwhile all around them—all around all of us—is another conversation way more influential, where control and abuse and even violence are not vilified but glorified. In fact, we call it *leadership* and *strength* and *decisiveness*. We actually make heroes out of people whose actions sound a lot like those of people we call criminals, batterers, and wife beaters; people we put in jail. But while abusers wreak havoc at home, some people we most admire pull it off on a much grander scale around the world and they aren't jailed. **They are rewarded and the message that abuse pays is not lost on anyone.**

It's not a good time

A researcher friend of mind approached me once and asked if he could evaluate my counseling program. In other words, he wanted to know whether what I was doing was working. Are the men coming out of my program doing better than they had been going in? Are they less violent, less controlling and less dangerous when they complete the program, which is, after all, the point? So, although my friend's request was not at all unreasonable, I had to tell him no. I said:

Look, this isn't a good time to evaluate my work to end violence. Just look around! Our leaders, with lots of help from their influential friends, have been using abusive power quite effectively and are getting away with it, too, lock, stock and barrel. Hardly anybody has been held to account for bad behavior in any way that might make him or her stop.

Winning, being right no matter what, and keeping total control are pretty popular ideas these days; lots of people have been trying them out. With that sort of a to-do list, how can I be held responsible for changing anybody? Besides, violence has been going on for as long as we have been here on this planet. Nobody—not kings, diplomats, philosophers, psychologists, scientists, nor any practitioner of any religion—has ever figured out how to stop it. That's why now isn't a good time to evaluate my work.

He couldn't help but agree.

If in fact we are surrounded by abusive culture, it is unwise and even unfair to evaluate programs that deal with individual men because no matter how hard we work, the culture—largely unseen but nonetheless impactful—will always win out. Abusive culture goes merrily on and a few counselors in a basement classroom with a raggedy piece of chalk promoting alternatives to violence cannot possibly change that.

On the other hand, it's not the culture itself that's violent. Rather, it's people in the culture who are violent. Culture can't join an abuser group and choose another life path, but an individual person modeling the culture certainly can. The challenge for us is that we have to work on two levels at once. We have to work at the level of culture—changing the abusive mindset that surrounds us—and we have to change the people for whom that mindset is their main model. The better we understand abusers, the more we understand abusive culture. The more we understand abusive culture, the more we will be able to challenge it. The story of abuse definitely needs telling, but not just a part of it—it must be the whole story.

Native Americans have a beautiful and apt proverb about the power of culture. With some embellishment, it goes like this:

> There was once a big forest filled with beautiful trees. One day, some trees began to feel unwell. Over time, more and more began to sicken. Some even died. All of the trees were worried, so a few brave trees got together and decided that they should leave the forest and seek out treatment for themselves. They made their way to the tree detox center and there they got 30 days of fresh air, sunshine, water and fertilizer and by the end of the 30 days, they felt wonderful and were anxious to make their way back to their forest home.

> When they returned, they greeted their old tree friends and put their restored roots back into the ground. But then, inexplicably, they began to feel sick

24

again and they weren't alone in their illness. Many trees in the forest were sick. But why? What did they have in common other than being trees?

Well, it turned out that the soil in which they and all of the others had been growing for so long was the real source of their troubles. It wasn't the trees themselves after all, at least not entirely; it was the soil in which they lived that transmitted the disease and infected them. It was *contagious*. The trees were the carriers.

Now the problem, seen from a new vantage point, looks different; clearly treating a few trees with sunshine and water, while necessary, will not be enough. No matter how many trees get fixed up, the problem will never go away so long as the soil in which they grow keeps making them sick. When something is contagious and that something is unwanted, we know what to do: Take immediate action to stop it in its tracks.

Focusing on the abusive culture allows us to see what the problem of abuse and violence is really all about and look at the question of causation from a different perspective. When viewed through the lens of culture, we can more clearly see that abuse and violence are, generally, not about mental illness or anger or drunkenness or irrationality or the personality problems of a few. Violent, abusive behaviors are often thought out, purposeful and deployed as a strategy to obtain and hold onto power in a culture that values power and control above all else. In fact, the tactics in pursuit of power are universal and with few exceptions have been employed since time began by those wanting to "get more."

The title of this chapter, *How to Get More*, has a double meaning—it's actually paradoxical. Abusers want more, as in power, but don't realize that their method of getting more leads to their getting less. Every action designed to further their power reduces it, by definition. In fact, the search for power is endless. I know that people who have lived with abusers understand precisely what I mean. For many abusers, nothing is ever enough because nobody ever experiences total power—there is always someone with more.

Our abusive leadership and those with whom they associate also want *more*, even when they clearly have enough. And they, too, are tragically fooled by the pursuit of it. The search for power and money never ends, no matter how rich and powerful they may become. We all know people like that— in search of a destination that cannot ever be reached. Unfortunately, in their pursuit to get more, they cause harm to the rest of us.

The *more* needs to be reframed; it needs a new understanding. If it had one and if it was widely shared, a lot of unnecessary misery might be prevented, a lot more happiness might be created, and the idea of *potential* might come to really mean something. Until then, we will mince no words. Abusers destroy families and often, ultimately, themselves. They tear apart entire communities for many generations and cost all of us enormously. Sometimes with a lot of effort, the victims can recover. But sometimes the damage is too great and we can't put those people back together again. *We need only look at families who experience violence and see what happened to them in order to know what could to happen to us.* People with this abusive mentality are destructive to themselves and others. And it's not always easy—or even possible—to fix what they have broken.

The region I live in is known for rich farmland—some of the best in the world—but most of it is now gone, replaced by strip malls and gas stations. We'll never get it back. Such mindless, mostly self-centered development that serves only a few at the expense of many is hard to turn around. But it is precisely that situation that confronts us now in the spread of unfettered control and violence. I am proposing that we consider how, where, when and by whom this abusive culture is promoted and, once exposed—once seen for what it truly is and might become—address it in all its manifestations. The abusive worldview is contagious, that's true, but we can inoculate ourselves against it. *All is not lost.*

Chad and Marsha: A usual example

Many women have said that their abusive partners originally made them feel as if they were different from other women. Marsha knew that Chad abused other women, but she didn't believe that he would ever abuse her. He even said as much, telling her that she was special, unlike those other bad women he had been forced to *correct*. It felt good to Marsha to be so appreciated and she never took it for granted. She always tried hard to please Chad because she never wanted to disappoint him. She always wanted to be in his good graces.

27

But Chad, like other abusers, *never* intended for that to be the case. Placing Marsha on a pedestal was mostly a cynical tactic and he was fully prepared to start knocking her off once he was confident that he had her trust and confidence, that her guard was down, and that his power position was secure.

When Chad began to find fault with Marsha, she blamed herself. She presumed that she had done something wrong. After all, he used to admire her. It *must* be her fault. She *must* have changed. In fact, Chad was using a bait and switch strategy, promising one thing but doing another. If only she had known.

The moral of the story is that being placed on a pedestal is never a good thing in the end and a definite warning sign of bad things to come.

Arguably, all politicians, our unusual suspects included, promise one thing and do another. People expect that from them, more or less. But in the 2016 US Presidential election, a smallish group of people, mostly not rich, nor well educated—the so-called 'left behind'—felt *very* special. They became part of a club where all the members were winners and where they could and did give expression to their worst impulses. It must have been rewarding to be one of that group at a Trump rally, threatening and denigrating others, such as protesters, the press and minority groups of all kinds, and to be totally immune from consequences of those once unacceptable behaviors. These people—Trump people—gleefully identified with their wealthy, winning candidate. He treated them well. He told them how great they were. He told them that they were going to be winners, just like him very, very soon. He was quite convincing and they believed every word of it. It remains to be seen whether they will get what they were promised.

Chapter 3

Tactics of Power and Control

Tactic \ `tactic\ n. 1: A device for accomplishing an end.
2. A method of employing forces in combat.

Every ten years or so, the U.S. needs to pick up some
small crappy little country and throw it against the
wall just to show the world we mean business.

— Michael Ledeen

Tactics is the term we use in the domestic violence field
to describe the actions abusers take in pursuit of power
and control. But it's really just a way to describe bad behavior.
Abusive acts always arise within a particular context—that
is to say, they are always purposeful. In that way, violence is
not the real aim, it's just one strategy of many that abusers
use to achieve a larger objective.

Most of the abusers I've worked with have an uncanny
mastery of these tactics and use them to very good effect.
They use them so well and so consistently that I've actually
wondered whether they had all read from the same book,
like *The Prince* or *The Art of War*. How, I've asked myself,
could all of these situations be so eerily similar? How do
they all know so well how this is done? Why do their stories

all sound the same? I was genuinely puzzled until it occurred to me that the desire for power and an understanding of the tactics and behaviors necessary to maintain it, are not the exclusive province of domestic abusers. They are actually universal and very common. Therefore, reading a 'How to Get More Power' book is not really necessary when our everyday culture provides all the instruction anyone needs.

In this section, I'll review the most common tactics and bad behaviors used to gain power and control. I'll show you how they are employed by domestic violence abusers—our usual suspects—and then look to where else we have seen such tactics before. How have our *unusual* suspects used them and to what ends?

Note that this is by no means a complete list of tactics—it's far from that. But it makes the point that when we see these behaviors out in the world, we will remember that they are deliberately used by abusive people to get what they want despite who might get hurt in the process. When we start to wonder whether this or that act can be thought to be abusive, we ought to ask at least these questions: What is motivating that bad behavior? What beliefs underlie it? What are the effects? Who benefits from it?

As I said, I could fill a book with examples of bad behaviors used for such purposes, but since we don't have time to waste, I will highlight just a few. I am sure that most of you will be able to come up with plenty of your own.

Abusive tactics

*Keep secrets and be stealthy. Tell lies—even
outrageous ones—almost all the time. Play the
savior. Play the victim. Claim it takes two to tango.
Impose double standards. Degrade and dehumanize.
Control information. Make people feel crazy. Control
resources. Create a good spin to explain it all away.*

Stealth

Once, as I was standing outside my house, I glanced up and
saw, to my surprise, what looked like a giant bat overhead—
like something out of *Star Wars*. Darth Vader? No, it was
a stealth bomber. "How," I wondered, "could *that* thing go
anywhere undetected? How in the world could something
so big, so ominous, so scary, not be seen for what it is?" *It
conceals itself, sending out no signals that reveal its true identity,
suggest its direction, or betray its deadly intent.*

"Stealth" is a perfectly apt word to describe how batterers get
away with their own, more local brand of abuse. I can't tell
you the number of times I've heard a man who's been revealed
as a batterer described by his neighbors and coworkers as an
honest, pillar-of-the-community kind of guy. Why? Because
such men have learned how to sound pretty upstanding,
mostly honest and even principled. Like the shadowy stealth
bomber, they have learned how to lurk beneath our radar.

Abusers don't come with warning labels. Women don't wind
up with them because they recognized them for what they
really are. They picked them to be their boyfriends and

husbands for what they pretended to be. Few women would say to their families or girlfriends over lunch, "You know the kind of guy I'm looking for? I want a man who'll abuse me, degrade me, erode my self-esteem and trust in other people, and instill in me enough self-doubt to convince me that I'm crazy. I hope to find a man who will trap me financially, isolate me emotionally, harm me physically, and maybe even kill me one day. I want a man I can be afraid of most of the time." No, women don't pick abusers. They pick men who have disguised themselves and their motives well enough to be largely undetectable.

Of course, domestic abusers mostly deceive and disguise themselves in private, to the detriment of their families. But other more powerful sorts deceive, too. It's just that the consequences of their abuse reach a lot further. Both groups use stealth and obfuscation to fool people into thinking that what is bad is good and what is wrong is right. And some do it very well.

Former director of the Christian Coalition, Ralph Reed, coined an unsettling phrase that has become widely known today: *stealth politics*. Stealth politics is the tactic of cloaking oneself (usually a candidate or elected official) and one's true purposes in language and public imagery that disguise those purposes. It's a strategy of sending out no signals that would clue people in to who you really are and what you're up to. It's a plan to fool people into thinking that you mean something or intend something that you, in fact, do not. In other words, "stealth" offers an effective way to further one's agenda without anyone noticing what you are really up to.

Recently, lots have wondered why so many people seemed to vote against their own interest and so enthusiastically support leaders who were their obvious antagonists. Like victims of violence, who are frequently blamed for staying with and remaining loyal to abusive men, those people were, and are, implicitly and even overtly labeled as being either totally ignorant or self-defeating or just plain bad, because they voted for causes and candidates that injured their wellbeing (and ours). But maybe they do so not because they are stupid or psychologically disordered (although I guess some likely are) but because they believe what sounds like a very credible argument. They are taken in, fooled by the manipulations and machinations of people with a self-serving and often well-hidden agenda. The camouflage works as intended.

Even professionals who work with abusive men admit that they have been fooled into believing an abuser's story that he is actually an upstanding person who did nothing wrong, only to discover at some later point that the story has more than a few holes in it. Knowing the difference between what is true and what isn't comes with some high stakes—whether in an abuser's home or outside of it. We, therefore, need to get it right most of the time.

Men who abuse and get away with it do so by successfully denying, minimizing and justifying their actions. They demand that their partners forget the past whenever it does not fit with the image they want people to hold of them or otherwise interferes with their present plans. They offer innocent explanations for their behavior that their victims are expected to accept. They patronize, appease, disguise and distract. And of course, they lie. That leaves people with misleading or even false information, a state of affairs that works well for abusers but badly for everybody else, making it ever harder to tell just what and whose agenda is being promoted.

In American politics, the Tea Party is commonly known to be a right-wing-funded project with a right-wing agenda. At least some of the people who were recruited to attend their rallies and town halls had no idea what or whom they were backing. In a now-iconic photograph, a Tea Party protester is holding up a sign that says 'Keep your government hands off my Medicare,' obviously not realizing that Medicare *is* the government. That is just one example of someone following along with a stealthy political group without realizing exactly what they are fighting against.

But it's not just single instances of political stealth. In fact, most of us no longer know whose selfish interests are being advertised under the guise of the common good. These days, we can't tell a legitimate public service announcement from a selfish, money-grabbing ploy, and all of that concealment makes it all but impossible to make good decisions about how we want our country to be run. Worse, the names people give these selfish agendas are very good at covering them up, and in fact, are deliberately designed to fool us.

There are so many examples of these stealthful names that to list them all would require ten books—and big ones at that—but here are a few examples just to make the point. *Americans for Prosperity* and *Freedom Works* are, or were, actually billionaire-funded organizations designed to prop up the fossil fuel industry and make even more money for the Kochs and others like them. Republican message strategists figured out the ultimate in stealth tactics when they came up with the *Clean Skies Initiative*, which was arguably about, guess what, allowing more pollution in the air. *The Healthy Forest Initiative* included cutting down trees, and years ago I had some interactions with a group called *Parents and Children Together Successfully* (PACTS) which was an organization dedicated to helping abusers lawfully wrest custody of children away from their mothers.

Generally, transparency is not a friend of domestic violence. If everybody really understood what was going on in an abusive home, it might stop. If people understood what the above organizations were really doing, they would no longer fly under the radar. Secrecy is a necessary ingredient in advancing the abusive worldview both in the home of an abuser and out in the world where a lack of disclosure creates confusion for everyone. It's hard to hold anyone accountable when we can't be exactly sure of what they have done. All of this stealth leaves us not knowing who or what to believe and not knowing who or what is real. When all information is suspect, everything is just opinion. And that makes for dangerous times.

In the domestic violence field, we teach people how to spot someone potentially abusive and how to avoid being fooled or taken in by an abuser masquerading as someone altogether innocent. If it's too late and a person is already involved with an abuser, we help that person to assess options and, if they desire, plan an escape. We need—but clearly lack—a similar assessment mechanism on a national scale. When the 'wrong' people assume power or gain a wide audience, all kinds of havoc can result and the really bad consequences, yet unseen, will be all but impossible to avoid.

In the final pages of this book, we will review some warning signs that we are about to get involved with someone who is guided by the abusive worldview. If it's too late and we've already gotten ourselves ensnared, we will look at how we can *get out* with the least amount of damage.

Telling it like it isn't: Denial and lies

It's not a lie if you believe it.

— George Costanza, *Seinfeld*

One of the most popular words in the field of domestic violence is *denial*. We use it all the time. We say that a person is *in denial* about their abuse. But what does that actually mean? People often ask me and other professionals about this tendency of abusive men to deny that they acted badly or did something wrong. Do they actually believe they didn't do those things? What does it mean when abusers claim to be innocent of an act that five people saw them do? Were they really *deluding themselves*, or were they just lying to get out of the consequences? When they claim that they didn't do it or that it wasn't their fault or that it was just an accident, *is that denial or is it a lie?*

When people misuse their power and exploit others, there is always a chance that someone will find out and the abuser will get called on the carpet for it and held to account. But accountability is rather limiting. How can an abuser continue to do whatever he wants if people keep asking him to explain himself? If he wants to operate without consequences, he needs a good explanation—one tried and tested. Although I have heard some wonderfully creative explanations and many can be found in my first book, *Ditch that Jerk*,[7] in general, these explanations fall into of one of the following categories: Deny that it happened at all; deny that you did it; deny that you meant to do it; claim that you *had* to do it; or say that nobody got hurt anyhow. In other words, deny your actions, deny your intentions, or deny the consequences. And sometimes do all three—that's how domestic abusers operate.

But what about our unusual suspects? Are *they* in denial? Or are they just lying, too? Do they really believe that giving all our tax dollars to rich people will make everyone better? Do they really believe that there is no such thing as climate change? Do they really believe that the earth is only 7000 years old? Do they really believe that it's no problem to dump coal waste into our streams? Do they actually believe that ending health care for 24 million people is a good thing or that Russia's shenanigans are just a hoax manufactured by liberals? Do they really believe that everyone would be safer if we all carried a gun? *Or is that just what they say to justify their actions?*

Just as we give a break to domestic abusers, assuming that they are in denial about their abuse and unaware of what they are doing or why, we give similar breaks to many of our unusual suspects by conceding that maybe they *do* believe these things on principle and aren't just using them for political and personal gain. That matters because standing on principle and acting out of self-interest might look the same but are very different animals. Professionals in domestic abuse intervention never let the abuser get away with such spin for long because if he is not challenged and he gets away with explaining his behavior away, he will never stop.

But what about our unusual suspects? MSNBC's Rachel Maddow stated in a very exasperated fashion one evening that the then-President-elect just lied to our faces. It was a whopper and it seemed like she could hardly believe it— although, she is much less surprised today. Many more lies followed—great big ones, too—and there were so many coming from so many places that they could scarcely be tracked.

Trump's budget director stated during a Senate hearing in early 2017, without any hesitation at all, that Medicaid was not going to be cut even though the Congressional Budget Office (CBO) score showed that it would be by close to a trillion dollars. A great big sign with actual numbers pronounced the truth. How did he explain and justify what was an obvious lie? He simply said that the CBO score might be wrong.[8] (*I didn't say that these excuses were good ones.*) In fact, reporters have taken to making and keeping lists of lies that emanate from the White House and elsewhere but it is a challenge to keep up. Lies are now as common—maybe more common—than the truth.

Whoppers that sound like the truth have become standard practice; they are definitely in vogue. There are so many that we are worn down, too tired to even challenge them anymore. And that's why they are still so popular in certain abusive circles.

(How to) save the town that doesn't need saving

1. Appear to "rescue" the target of abuse from herself, whether she genuinely needs saving or not, despite your being the cause of a lot of the trouble in the first place.

2. Create a crisis, cripple or destroy someone or something entirely, then proclaim the person or the program a total failure that must be saved from itself.

3. Ensure you benefit greatly from the so-called failure.

In old westerns, there is always a guy (never a woman, of course) who would ride into a town and save it from the bad guys who were holed up somewhere plotting and planning to take advantage of the naïve, powerless folk who live there. That town-saver exhibits all of the usual stereotypical masculine traits: He is a stand-alone guy; he does not go before the town council to ask for permission to wipe out the evil ones; nor does he care at all what anybody thinks. This myth is appealing and that is why it gets repeated over and over again in movies and television and games and everyplace else—it's a powerful force that pulls on our collective psyches. But for the myth to work and to endure, at least one major condition must be present—there must actually be a town that needs saving. That point cannot be overstated. A town that works well doesn't need saving and, therefore, doesn't need the hero. So, the town must first be destroyed so that a would-be hero will have something to save.

People who have lived with abusers tell us that they often have a *make you over* mentality. Abusers tell their victims repeatedly that they aren't good enough, that they are terrible, and that he, the abuser, will rescue them from their own debauchery and make them over into something better. Unfortunately, what often happens is that he completes the first part of his task, which is to destroy her self-esteem, her self-efficacy, and her confidence, but the second phase, where he supposedly will help her build herself into someone new, never materializes. He has destroyed her beyond the point where she can be made better.

This is a popular tactic of long standing among unusual suspects, too. Cripple something by cutting the funding to support it and render it totally ineffective, and then claim that it doesn't work and should be eliminated on the grounds that—guess what!—it doesn't work. Abusers know that creating a crisis or making a mess of some person, project, program or institution by harming them beyond repair through neglect or malevolent interference is a chance to start over and create something more to their liking. After all, it was no good to begin with. Destroying it just makes it better!

The Affordable Care Act (ACA) repeal and replace effort is the epitome of this tactic. Our abusive political leaders have been interfering with the program so that it falls apart, claiming that it's collapsing right in front of us and should, therefore, be destroyed and *made over*. But of course, it was them who supported (in fact, created) the conditions that caused it to fail in the first place. We were told that the ACA was collapsing as we speak. House Republicans then began what they called a "mission of mercy"—the Speaker of the House even claimed that they were "coming to the rescue," saving us all from something none of us really wants to be saved from.[9]

According to Republicans, they had *no choice* but to foist something horrific on us because the thing that they were destroying was already a goner anyhow—making it so was the plan all along. This tactic works well for both of our abuser sets. Destroy people and things with a promise to restore them, but never actually come through or produce the restoration part. Decimate something, blame it for what happens to it, and then walk away. Abusers are destructive— that's a plain fact. Whatever they involve themselves in will likely suffer—on both the home front and the world stage.

The Trump Administration's cabinet, arguably installed through a major upheaval known as *the election*, is largely made up of people who seem ready to destroy the very agencies they have been chosen to lead. The Administrator of the Environmental Protection Agency (EPA) has been suing that agency to roll back regulations on air and water pollution. The Secretary of Education, who is in charge of America's public schools, has been working for decades to destroy and replace them with private, for-profit ones. The Secretary of Health and Human Services, who is in charge of health care and other social programs, wants to severely limit those programs, thereby undermining many people's health. The Secretary of Energy once said he wanted to eliminate the Department of Energy altogether. The Department of State stands to eliminate most key staff and turned down a Congressional offer of many millions of dollars designed to fight Russian and ISIS propaganda. The person in charge of contraception policy doesn't believe that contraception works. And it goes on.

To many, it seems unreal that people who are hostile to their departments are now running them, but that's the point after all. It's a cynical ploy to consolidate power because the aforementioned—and many other—institutions are an impediment to an abuser's total control. The destroyers are in charge, claiming, in a crazy-making sort of way, that in order to save these organizations they must first be destroyed. In order to save education, we must ruin it. In order to save the EPA, we must neutralize it. In order to save Social Security and Medicare and Medicaid, we have to get rid of them. To protect civil and voting rights, we need to curtail them. And so it goes. If they continue on their *saving* mission, soon enough there won't be anything to left to save.

Domestic abusers destroy their families. Our abusive leaders will assuredly destroy our collective home—arguably, they have already started. Forget what they say. Ignore their pleas for understanding or agreement or forgiveness. Ignore their claims that everything is falling apart around us. Those are simply justificatory tactics. We have to see them for what they are and what they are really doing. We should listen closely when the Right tries to convince us that we need saving. Their *actual* aim is to make our destruction look like a rescue.

It takes two to tango

Another way abusers deal with the accusation that they have been abusive is to claim that there are two sides to every story. That way, people get confused about what really happened and at least some doubt is created as to whether the abuser was solely responsible for the abuse. Because this tactic is used so often, it creates doubt in the minds of people who hear the story. If you were to walk into any abuser group, you would hear from most participants the following: "She should be here too! She slapped me first! She is just as violent, but the man is always the one who gets arrested! There are two sides to every story!" I can state without exaggeration that the vast majority of people ordered to an abuser group will, at least initially if not throughout, tell us that it 'takes two to tango' and that they should not be held responsible— at least not solely responsible—for bad behavior. The tactic, when used successfully, allows the one who is causing the problem to keep right on doing it.

Climate change communication is but one very clear example of the successful use of this 'two sides' tactic by our unusual suspects. Climate change deniers, as they have come to be called, argue that the earth isn't warming and they point to a few scientists who have offered a competing theory. If they can't get away with saying that, they claim it's nobody's fault—it's a natural occurrence. They may also argue that it's just not that big a problem because soon enough we will be able to go to Mars or other planets, anyhow. They commonly assert that we need big oil jobs more than we need clean air and water and, in any case, there is nothing we can do about it. And what do we do when nothing can be done? Well, nothing, of course.

In some places, the 'two sides' tactic shows up in the rewriting of textbooks and curricula to suggest that evolution is just a theory and that there is another explanation for how we got here, which is the 'theory' of Creationism. Creationism ignores, or denies, the most obvious of evidence about the age of the earth. It is viewed by the right as another theory that deserves presentation and teachers in some schools in some red states are being required to teach it as if it were just another side that we must mull over. They have figured out that simply offering another side, no matter how outrageous or improbable, will work often enough.

When an abuser claims that there are two sides, the resulting investigation and seeking out of the truth can take some time. Often, there is no smoking gun and sometimes no evidence can be located; all that is available for review are what the two sides have said about it. It's a he said/she said situation and that frequently stops the case in its tracks. But sometimes there *is* a smoking gun.

In a 2017 Congressional campaign in Montana, then candidate and future Congressman Greg Gianforte, annoyed by a reporter's questions concerning the Affordable Care Act, attacked him, pushing him to the ground and breaking his glasses. Now, there were witnesses to the crime—at least three—and an audio of the whole thing, too. It was very clear what had happened and yet the candidate's spokesperson, Shane Scanlon, actually blamed the whole ugly incident on the victim, Ben Jacobs, and on liberals by saying, "It's unfortunate that this aggressive behavior from a liberal journalist created this scene at our campaign volunteer BBQ."[10]

A report in *The Guardian* tells us:

> Scanlon blamed Jacobs for the altercation, saying that he "entered the office without permission, aggressively shoved a recorder in Greg's face, and began asking badgering questions." "Jacobs was asked to leave," the statement reads. "After asking Jacobs to lower the recorder, Jacobs declined. Greg then attempted to grab the phone that was pushed in his face. Jacobs grabbed Greg's wrist, and spun away from Greg, pushing them both to the ground."[11]

The Congressman later pled guilty in a court of law.

In any abuser group, this kind of convoluted, twisted and implausible story—such as the one offered by the Congressman's spokesperson, designed to make the victim look equally bad—is a common one; anybody who works with domestic abusers would have recognized their denial and excuses immediately. In fact, in many instances there are not two sides to the abuser's story. There is only one side. The abuser did, in fact, abuse somebody. The Congressman did attack a reporter. The climate is changing. Creationism isn't a scientific theory. And no amount of outlandish storytelling makes any of that any different.

According to David Brock in *The Republican Noise Machine*, this well-organized and relentless campaign has been going on for a long time and has largely succeeded "by turning the news—once a bastion of objectivity—into a he said/she said affair where there are few facts and mostly opinions."[12] In other words, everything becomes a matter of mere opinion. According to Brock, the news show formula was always to pair a non-partisan, objective reporter with a right-wing demagogue with an agenda:

> Every issue, observation, point and fact suddenly had another side: the right-wing side. If 99% of scientists agreed that the earth was round, while 1% said it was flat, the two views were given equal time and thus equal validity in the minds of the viewers.[13]

Yep, that's how it is done.

Some years ago, a men's rights activist called me up to ask whether my public presentations about domestic violence were fair and balanced. I asked him naively, "What do you mean, 'balanced?'" He replied that he wondered whether I made a particular point to note that women are as violent as men. I laughed. "Why would I want to say that," I responded calmly, "It isn't true." He didn't take my refusal very well because it interfered with his "fair is only fair" tactic.

The usual suspects tell us regularly, "Hey, the man is always arrested, but the woman is just as guilty! Why isn't she in a court-ordered group? Why don't you people [domestic violence professionals] ever talk about how women are just as violent? This isn't fair!" By making violence seem to be just some universal relationship problem, carriers of the ideology of violence can skirt the real issue and dodge accountability.

It's just a little spat

People often say to couples in relationships where there is abuse that they should try harder to get along. They refer to what goes on between them as simple bickering, with both people sharing blame, even when the situation is far worse than a mere spat. But what people fail to understand is that abusers benefit greatly from these minimizations and their 'just get along' admonitions. Naturally, they encourage that kind of characterization about their behavior because the people they abuse are less likely to protest their treatment or fight back lest they be accused of being the problem themselves. When people acquiesce to the abuser's demands, as they often do, things may, in fact, become more peaceful.

But that only conceals the reality and doesn't make any of it any less destructive.

We have also heard the term 'partisan bickering' to refer to the relationship between political leaders on either side of the aisle. We hear that they should try harder to work together and that if they could all just get along, government would be more peaceful and effective. While it's inarguable that if they all worked together in good faith things would undoubtedly improve, the point is that authoritarian environments are usually peaceful and conflict free. People are well-controlled and behaved, all in ostensible agreement, never speaking out. But of course, that that does not reflect the reality either; people have just suppressed what they really feel. Democratic, egalitarian societies and families where there is greater equality are messy—lots of people have lots of strong opinions and they voice them. Not so in dictatorships. Everybody just 'gets along.'

'Getting along' is often then a code word for 'getting the victim to be quiet in the face of abusiveness,' thereby giving the abusive person(s) free reign and total control. When I was in college, we would have termed that kind of suppression a 'hegemonic discourse,' which, simply means that those in power have a way of talking and framing ideas that is designed to help them maintain their power and keep people in their places. Telling people that they should be nice—the equivalent of telling women to smile more—is a perfect example of it.

Not the Usual Suspects

The so-called resistance movement, which arrived around the time of Trump's election, has loudly opposed the actions of abusive political leaders, something to which those leaders are not accustomed and would prefer to see stopped. Many have become afraid to go to their offices or hold town hall meetings because so many people show up and want to be heard. Consequently, calls to 'just get along' have increased, coming mainly from our unusual, abusive political leaders who see it as a way to *self-silence* us. That suggestion— be nicer—were we to follow it, only disadvantages the resistance, which is finally, fully speaking up, and it further emboldens those attempting to 'get more,' who really don't want to hear us. Here is a takeaway idea: Blaming victims or holding them responsible for making peace and getting along is a *tactic of abuse, not a solution.*

Like the domestic abuser, many of our unusual suspects claim that that there are two sides to everything; it's a he said/she said world. Maybe they believe it. Maybe they don't. Either way, it interferes with our ability to understand what's really happening to us and make good decisions for ourselves.

Double standards and false equivalencies

*I just don't see how our stories compare—I was so bad
because I wore sweats and left shoes around and didn't
keep a perfect house or comb my hair the way you
liked it—or had dinner ready at the precise moment
you walked through the door or that I just plain got
on your nerves sometimes. I just don't see how that
compares to infidelity, wife beating and verbal abuse.*

— Nicole Brown Simpson

One way an abuser invokes accountability or responsibility is to attach it to someone other than him or herself. In other words, they want to hold other people to standards that they don't apply to themselves. Rules and standards of behaviors are for the other guy. The point is to make their bad behavior look no worse than the person they have harmed, even though their behavior may be very much worse in both intent and effect. Being messy or losing one's keys or wearing sweatpants is not the same as repeated strikes against a person's self-esteem, ongoing expressions of contempt or physical violence.

A common and effective way to express the double standard is to project out onto others one's own fears and perceived shortcomings and then ruthlessly attack them. The tactic calls for abusers to blame someone else for what they themselves have done or thought about doing. Lots of these men lie to their partners and cheat on them. And what do you suppose invokes their greatest ire? It's the perception that their partners are cheating and lying. As with almost all abusive men, much of what they hate and rail against is what they, themselves, do with remarkable consistency. Nearly every action that outrages them is a perfectly formed example of the exact thing they do to others. The tactic to 'turn the tables' is projection and hypocrisy.

Jacques Ellul, an ethicist studying and writing about propaganda, writes:

> He who wants to provoke a war will not only proclaim his own peaceful intentions but also accuse the other party of provocation. He who uses concentration camps accuses his neighbors of doing so. He who intends to establish a dictatorship insists that his adversaries are hell bent on dictatorship. And, he who makes the accusation first always appears somehow purged, even if he is worse. The propagandist will not accuse the enemy of just any misdeed; he will accuse him of the *very intention that he himself has and of trying to commit the crime that he himself is about to commit.*[14]

Perhaps that is why abusive men claim so often that their partners are violent. If we believed even half of what these men said about their wives' violence, we would be forced to conclude that, in fact, the women start it all and are actually more violent, by a mile, than their husbands and boyfriends ever thought about being. And that's the point of their particular brand of propaganda.

In one case, a woman was so severely beaten that she was hospitalized for three weeks. As she was being wheeled into the ambulance, the abuser told the police standing by that if she pressed charges he would too, because she slapped him first and he had a very slight red mark on his cheek. The policeman turned to the injured woman and said, "Well, if he wants to press charges, I will have to arrest you. Do you still want to go forward?" The woman, concerned about how such a charge would affect her employment, said no and her abuser walked away, off the hook. Even though there was simply no comparison in terms of the harm, the abuser was successful in turning the tables and making it look like it was the same thing.

Abusive men know that it's important to get their accusations, even when fabricated, out there first. It is a preemptive first strike and it can be very effective. For example, as courts began issuing restraining orders to protect victims, *ex parte* (without the defendant present), abusers discovered that it'd be a good tactic to get to the courthouse first. They would go to see the judge, allege that they were the ones who had been abused, and then when the actual victim arrived to ask for the court's help and protection, she would look defensive, like she was trying to pull a fast one. "She threw a shoe at me first, Your Honor," the abuser might say, "Can I help it if I had to respond?"

An example of the double standard—hypocrisy, by any other name—is the much-hyped demand for "fair and balanced" news and commentary, which has resulted in a virtual absence of any fact-based news on *Fox*. The vitality of a democracy absolutely depends on the objectivity of its media, but, interestingly, when Matt Labash, then senior editor of Rupert Murdoch's right-wing *Weekly Standard*, was asked in 2003 why conservative outlets, such as *Fox*, have become so popular, he replied:

> We've created this cottage industry in which it pays to be unobjective...It's a great way to have your cake and eat it, too. Criticize other people for not being objective. Be as subjective as you want. It's a great little racket. I'm glad we found it, actually.[15]

I bet.

Donald Trump and his supporters, including *Fox*, have been calling actual news fake so that people will stop listening. However, in the summer of 2017, it was revealed that *Fox* likely conspired with the Trump administration to manufacture (make up) a story to make the Democrats look bad.[16] They retracted the story, because they were caught red-handed. The point is that while Trump and some *Fox* anchors were accusing real news of being fake, they were busy creating and disseminating actual fake news in keeping with their usual approach.

These techniques are on full and continuous display. In fact, there are plenty of examples of double standards in our political system, but one stands out: Congress voted to exempt themselves from the Affordable Care Act repeal![17] They would take health care away from everyone, while keeping it themselves. Only when the press discovered their plan did they have to give it up. Exposure, exposure, exposure.

The entire 2016 US Presidential election, and unfortunately beyond, is a study in the repeated and successful use of these techniques. It was a classic 'get there first and pre-empt the accusations from the other side.' For example, Hillary Clinton was accused of having conflicts of interest because of her role in the Clinton Foundation and likewise was accused of endangering our national security because her emails could have been hacked. As it turned out, the other candidate had enormous and disturbing ongoing conflicts of interest, along with a likely connection to, if not involvement in, extensive foreign hacking, or much worse. But Trump and his group pre-empted Clinton's accusations—he got there first. Yes, maybe she threw a shoe, but Trump dragged her by the hair outside the house, punched her in the face and made her fear for her life.

Playing the victim

Feigning victimhood, believe it or not, is a tactic designed to take and maintain control. In abuser groups, we constantly see men present themselves and their stories as if they were the real victims.

In every group I've worked with, many of the participants recite—or would if we allowed it—a litany of how they have been wrongly treated by their wives, the system, everybody— it's rare for abusive men to talk about how their partners have been badly treated or have suffered. Although some do manage to make the connection between their violence and their family's misery, not many will. Most just feel put upon by the courts, cops and prosecutors—who collectively have the audacity to hold him accountable for his actions—and by the very people they have themselves victimized: their wives and children. The abusers matter, but their families don't.

Why would a person who seemingly holds all the cards choose to portray himself as a victim? There are credible psychological explanations for that tendency, which are real and I don't discount them, but the other reason to employ victimhood, particularly as our unusual suspects use it, is because it is astonishingly effective. For instance, a claim of victimhood deflects criticism, elicits sympathy more often than blame, dilutes the negative consequences that might accrue to someone who is guilty (victims don't get punished), and is a great misdirection. It also mobilizes support and creates anger—an anger that is necessary to fire up supporters and allies. That is not to say that some don't come to believe their own stories of victimhood. In fact, the way in which they view the world—the abusive worldview—leads to that kind of thinking.

That worldview is built around ideas of dominance, hierarchy and absolute power that can never be achieved, let alone sustained. In trying never to be a victim of anything, they wind up being victims of everything. All of our suspects have figured out how to use victimhood to their advantage. When they have no obvious claim to victimhood, they make something up. The so-called War on Christmas, used incessantly by *Fox* and other right-wing pundits, is a prime example. *Fox News* led the way in the promotion of what is now known as grievance culture—an incessant, non-stop complaining about bad, unfair treatment at the hands of liberals. According to journalist and author Thomas Frank, victimhood is the *raison d'être* of conservatives. He writes:

> Understanding themselves as victims besieged by a hateful world absolves conservatives of responsibility for what goes on around them. It excuses their failings; it justifies the most irresponsible rages; and it allows them, both in public and private life, to resolve disputes by pointing their fingers at the outside world and blaming it all on the depraved liberal elite.[18]

These grievances provide a tidy justification for abusive behavior.

Many years ago, I heard a right-wing, anti-feminist commentator, whose name long ago vanished from my mind, make a lot of to-do about a tongue-in-cheek Father's Day card he'd seen that, he thought, unfairly targeted men. The card posed the question: "Men—can we live better with them or without them?"

When I first heard his complaint, I was astounded. Did he really mean to suggest that men are treated as badly as women in the world? Who was he kidding? I've worked with real victims and I'm pretty sure that not one of them would have much to say about getting dissed in a greeting card. Their concerns range more toward being stalked, being perennially afraid and feeling hopeless and unworthy. He couldn't possibly mean to suggest that a comment on a greeting card approaches the abuse millions endure every day around the world. But alas, he most certainly did mean it. In the end, all he got to be was a *greeting-card victim.* Now that's a false equivalency if ever there was one.

Regardless of the severity of their claims, the domestic abuser points to his family, the courts, the system and the world and cries, "I am the victim! The system is rigged against me. I am just not being treated right," all the while wielding enormous and often toxic power over his family. The carriers of abusive ideology do the same; they claim to be victims while wielding enormous power over the entire country and even the world. I am certain we can find enough examples of this tactic among our unusual suspects to fill up the state of Texas.

Degrading and dehumanizing

Is there a connection between what we say about people and what we do to them? I mean, does how we talk about individuals or groups of people affect how we think of them and, ultimately, how we treat them? If we call women pigs, for instance, are we more or less likely to treat them badly? It takes little expert analysis to know the answer to that question. In fact, most abuse starts in the "innocent" realm of language. It starts with sarcasm, put-downs and disparagements and ends with physical injury, psychological trauma and sometimes death.

Abusers are notorious for the ugly language they use with and about their partners. Abuser groups ring out with words like *crazy, bitch, whore, fat, lazy, ugly, stupid* and so on. By saying those things about his partner, he creates for himself a kind of permission to treat her badly. He creates an environment within which bad behavior is excused and acceptable. In offender groups, men are always asked to refer to their wives by name and to refrain from calling them 'the wife,' the 'old lady,' and so on. That's because it matters that the abuser sees his wife as a person and not as an object. How we describe someone affects how we deal with him or her.

If a victim is being disparaged, she should take that seriously because that's how abuse of a more sinister and harmful nature starts. Terrible behavior rarely happens without any warning at all. It begins with these kinds of put-downs and degradations. People who are told how worthless they are—how unimportant and insignificant—often eventually come to agree. They start to believe it.

Men in abuser groups are keenly aware of this propensity and they use it to their victim's detriment. They understand that to be referred to over and over as lazy or crazy or dumb takes its toll. Victims come to believe the story about how terrible they are and may begin to act as if it were true. We call that a self-fulfilling prophesy. Even women who came into a relationship feeling relatively good about themselves will, after enough degradation, conclude that they really are bad and that they deserve bad treatment.

The public airwaves, along with the general environment, have become threatening, abusive, and frightening. It's all the rage to be insulting and derogatory. It's tempting to blame a few people for the escalation of this uncivilized mass communication, but in fact it's been going on for many years. What we see today is merely the predictable result and inevitable culmination of decades of incivility. The 2016 election was, at first, shocking. Were people really insinuating that small hands meant a small penis? Were people really being called *crooked, little* and *dumb?* The name-calling and belittling that characterized the election was once confined to the fringe, but because it was never challenged, tolerance for it grew and meanness worsened and spread. It's like an abuser's behavior, which, when it goes unchecked, always *escalates.*

Right-wing radio is notorious for inflammatory, vicious rhetoric. Radio talk show host Michael Savage once referred to liberals as sewer rats[19] while Rush Limbaugh has repeatedly called women feminazis and once even likened Chelsea Clinton to the family dog.[20] Others have compared Michele Obama to a gorilla[21] while religious leader Pat Robertson infamously blamed gays for 9/11, claiming it was God punishing America for allowing them to march in a parade.[22] White supremacists have been vocal and vulgar and these few examples, of many thousands, are actually on the tame side of what's been circulating for decades. We shouldn't be surprised that it eventually showed up in a Presidential debate.

A favored tactic of the abuser, insulting and undermining someone in very personal and even vicious ways, is now regular, everyday behavior. Some of the put-downs are blatant and vile. Others are subtle but nonetheless contemptible. Either way, they sink in. We get it. A major warning sign, we should pay attention when our leaders use their power to disparage because violence or other unpleasant consequence frequently follows.

Controlling information

> *The sooner the print press goes away the*
> *better it will be for society.*

> —Paul LePage,
> Governor of Maine

People need to be able to trust someone or something, otherwise it's a free for all. It has been extensively reported that few of us Americans place our trust in institutions or traditions anymore. We don't trust politicians, government or the media. We certainly don't trust corporations and we don't even trust each other. Once trust in everything is eroded, people naturally look more readily to anyone who seems to know the truth. Because widespread distrust is naturally isolating, it provides a super opportunity for an authoritarian to enter the mix, clear it all up, and give us something to believe in. Abusers and authoritarian leaders of every stripe around the world know this well and so, between both suspect groups, isolation is a primary strategy.

For domestic abusers, isolation as a tactic is simply a given. For example, many work hard to make sure that their wives are distanced, physically and/or emotionally, from friends and family. Friends and family can be supportive and a good source of esteem-retaining information, which the abusive man does not want his partner to hear. They might suggest to her in a convincing manner that there is a life apart from the control of the abuser, so he wants to ensure that he is the one and only source of information.

Many of the men I've worked with over the years have tried keeping their partners out of the world. They'd prefer that they not have jobs or talk to people too much or otherwise find out what's really going on. They are afraid that their partners might become educated, discover other options and leave. Of course, the concerns are well-founded. Once people figure out that the way they have been living and the manner in which they are being treated is neither normal nor necessary, they want something else. Isolating people from a full range of information, whether overtly and physically or in more subtle and sinister ways, is an effective tactic.

I need hardly say that what is happening in American politics today mirrors this description precisely. A new President berated and attacked reporters, degrading them by calling them bad and awful enemies of the people and totally dishonest. Many feared for their safety. And he isn't alone; the press has been degraded by the right wing for many years. Any outside source of information that cannot be controlled is the natural antagonist of those who want to get more without interference.

Nothing more boldly stands in the way of total control for the few than the presence of people who are smart and educated, and who can figure out what's up. When people are paying attention and have the facts, it's much harder to pull the wool over their eyes. Therefore, it behooves the abuser to be the most important, if not the only, source of information. Donald Trump knew this when he said, "I love the poorly educated."[23] The poorly educated are not likely to challenge what the big guys do.

Misinformed people don't make good decisions in the voting booth or anyplace else, all of which works well for abusive political leaders who want us to keep quiet. When objective sources of information are gone, so is an important check on the proliferation of the abusive worldview and its carriers. We know that people who watch *Fox News* and listen to right-wing radio are not informed as to the actual facts. In fact, they know less than people who listen to nothing at all. In any dictatorship, there is a state-run media and the dictator controls what people hear. *Fox News* and their counterparts are like that; they are a source of propaganda which lots of people believe is the truth. Like an abuser's family, who come to believe whatever the abuser says and nothing that they hear from others, propaganda perpetuates the abusive worldview and gives ever more control to those who ought not have it.

A "poorly educated," distrustful, fearful, and economically desperate group of people are easy to control. If the press and other sources of credible information and influence are ever effectively silenced—because their integrity is damaged beyond repair and because people don't know what's real and what's fake anymore—there won't be two sides to any story. There will be only one and it will be theirs.

Crazy-making

*Deny that what happened really did happen, so the
victim doubts her own perceptions.*

It's common for abusive men to convince their victims
and others that they are not seeing what they are actually
seeing. In the domestic violence arena, it's called crazy-
making and its purpose is to cause a victim to question her
perception, thereby weakening and controlling her. When
our perceptions are repeatedly assaulted, we may not know
what is real anymore; we lose our grounding and are injured
psychologically. For example, I have known more than a few
domestic abusers who, after assaulting their partners, will
then tell them and others that she did it to herself. Not an
insignificant number of men actually report to authorities
that their wives beat themselves up. Worse, sometimes
victims will come to agree with the abuser's absurd
characterizations. It's not hard to imagine how that would
lead people to feel totally crazy. Abusers want their partners
to question themselves, not the abuser.

George Orwell wrote about this dynamic in his
groundbreaking classic book *1984*.[24] When people give up
what once may have been their reality in favor of the reality
of those wishing to control them, the controlling person—
the abuser—is victorious, his control cemented. Lies—even
ridiculous ones—continue to be offered up to us and they
serve as tactics for the abuser to gain more power. Some lies
are minor, without much consequence, such as the one that
Trump put forward about his inauguration crowd size being

bigger than Obama's.[25] There are also bigger ones such as when members of the Trump administration claimed that Medicaid would be not cut, even though they were cutting it at that moment.[26] Claiming that climate change is a hoax or that Russia did not interfere in our 2016 election are more along the lines of whoppers. There were a series of falsehoods, which came to be known in Orwellian fashion as 'alternative facts.'[27] Those alternative facts circulated widely and made lots of people absolutely crazy.

Even those who are not duped by all these 'alternative facts' are nonetheless very upset— psychologically and emotionally— by them. Injustice and lies that go unchallenged have a dispiriting effect on reasonable people. Unchallenged gross injustices tend to cause people to feel hopeless, helpless and depressed. What victims and their advocates endure—the consistent injustice; the lies the abuser tells and that other people believe; the inhumane ways in which the victims are characterized, blamed and held responsible, not just by the abuser but by a system that believes in him and less often in her—is analogous to what many Americans now feel, too.

When we no longer can tell the difference between up and down, true or false, we are made crazy and disbelieving of everything. A favored tactic of domestic abusers, crazy-making keeps people off balance, questioning their intuition about the abuser and often stuck in a bad situation from which extrication seems impossible, if not unthinkable. Those of us who have followed the propaganda from the unusual suspects wonder how they can say such things and how it is that formidable numbers of people believe them.

How can they get away with saying that there is no such thing as global warming or that evolution is merely an iffy theory? When we question everything and believe nothing, we are susceptible to the machinations of people with nefarious motives. And there are more than a few of those today.

There is a related concept that I want to mention: learned helplessness. Learned helplessness is a psychological condition sometimes associated with victims. Here's what it means: When people discover that nothing they do, no action they take, changes their condition whatsoever, they just stop trying. In other words, when all efforts are always in vain, they give up because nothing makes any difference anyway. They learn to be helpless and under the abusive culture, guess who benefits from that?

In the US, what most people want never happens. People vote (or try), and yet, for many, their candidate never wins. People protest mass killings and ask for stronger gun laws but none ever materialize. People want good, affordable and humane health care and yet the political leadership supports and passes a bill that fewer than 20% agree with. Less than a quarter of the country is responsible for the election of a person that the rest definitely don't support. The effect, if not the actual goal, is that we question our sanity and self-efficacy and become more compliant. But we aren't helpless—and we aren't crazy, either.

People think victims exaggerate what happened to them and make things up, which of course the abuser is glad to confirm. Sometimes, people just cannot believe what a victim tells them because it sounds so incredibly awful. They say, "Couldn't be! She must be crazy. That would never have happened," further increasing her sense of unreality.

Many have said similar things about the motives and actions of our unusual suspects. *They would never do that,* we say. *They wouldn't leave us without health insurance. They wouldn't cut Social Security. They wouldn't poison our water or give us thousands of fracking-induced earthquakes. They wouldn't sell us and our country down the river in order to enrich themselves. They wouldn't tell us one bald-faced lie after another. Would they?* How, we ask incredulously, *can they say things that are just patently false, if not bizarre, and how is it that formidable numbers of people believe them? How can they get away with saying that there is no such thing as global warming or that Donald Trump never lies? How can they state so confidently that which we know to be untrue? How can they lie to our faces repeatedly?* It's exasperating. And they know it.

Controlling resources:
The ultimate abuse tactic

*"No person, I think, ever saw a herd of buffalo, of
which a few were fat and the great majority lean. No
person ever saw a flock of birds of which two or three
were swimming in grease and the others
all skin and bones."*

—Henry George

The most obvious and even ubiquitous abusive behavior
in all suspects is the control of resources and the ways in
which that control is maintained and justified. Abusive men
frequently assert their power and control over their families
by deciding who gets what. That's pretty well understood by
most people as a tactic of abuse.

Rather than showing that controlling resources is a favored
tactic of abuse—that needs little additional explanation—I'd
like to use this section to expose those explanations for what
they really are: Justifications to avoid being held accountable
and to help our suspects get their way. I saved this part for
last because it combines a number of favored tactics rolled
up into one. Let's begin with a man in one of my groups,
Jerry, because his situation highlights the point.

One evening in my domestic violence group, some men were
complaining that their wives spend too much money. In fact,
it is quite common to hear men complain that their wives
have a spending problem. On this night, Jerry was telling the

group about how he had gotten angry with his wife, Jennifer, and had thrown some of her glass figurines against the wall. According to Jerry, Jennifer had been shopping at the dollar store and liked to buy little glass objects to decorate the house. On occasion, she would buy several per week. To Jerry, that level of spending was out of control. She did not need those things at all!

The real problem arose when Jennifer reminded him of his recent purchase of a four-wheeler and of his last two weekends out with his friends at the casino—neither were exactly needed and, when combined, set the family back a pretty penny. Even though they both worked and contributed, Jerry was enraged that Jennifer would question how he spent *his* money. He was the one with the full-time job. She just worked at a local restaurant. Although she worked hard, she made less. The family money was, therefore, in his view, his to spend as he pleased. He did not appreciate her tendency to buy things that she wanted—things he didn't want and to which he had not agreed.

Jerry described his wife in unflattering terms during every group. According to Jerry, his wife was lazy. He was the main breadwinner, after all, and she needed to remember that and behave in ways that showed him acknowledgment for it. Although she cooked the meals, cleaned the house and watched their two kids, making a very important contribution, Jerry saw her as a parasite; a taker. And he never failed to remind her and others of it.

Jerry never considered that he could not make as much money were it not for Jennifer taking care of everything else. In other words, *he did not do it alone* even though he liked to think that he did. Jerry believed that his wife should never be able to get her hands on his money. After all, he made it and he intended to keep it, sharing only what he saw fit. His freedoms, he believed, should not be infringed upon and his needs should be foremost. He felt entitled to and deserving of getting *more*, while Jennifer was deserving of less. *That's just how things are.* In the abusive worldview, it's true that greed and self-centeredness are actually spun into moral virtues—at the least they are not vices and getting your due is perfectly acceptable, regardless of what it does to somebody else.

We have heard over and over that whatever well-off people have, they made it entirely themselves and the government should never be allowed to get its hands on it. They should not have to contribute to the roads on which trucks haul their products, for example. They should not have to contribute to the courts that mediate their conflicts or the police that protect them. They deserve to keep what they've 'earned' for themselves, while everyone else contributes to and funds the very systems they've built their wealth on. Of course, there is nothing new to this belief. Over 100 years ago, an English essayist wrote the following, which is still quite relevant: "The poor have sometimes objected to being governed badly. The rich have always objected to being governed at all."[28]

In many areas, dollar stores are becoming ever popular. They go by names like Dollar General, Family Dollar, and

71

Dollar Tree. As the average family becomes less and less able to frequent restaurants and department stores, dollar stores become their saving grace. In so many towns, where a department store or restaurant once was, a dollar store now stands tall.

In stark juxtaposition to these very popular stores, which are increasing their customer base every day, are the people who would never set foot in such a place and likely have never even seen one before. These are the people, a relative few, who have so much that they couldn't possibly need more. As the argument goes, how many yachts does one really need? How many dinners can you eat? How fast does your car need to go when the speed limit is 55? Yet, by a number of accounts, those few people—the very wealthy, the never-dollar store crowd—are salivating at the prospect of *getting more* through Republican proposed tax cuts that are being promoted and promised to them by the unusual suspects in political leadership. Those cuts will need to come from someplace. Many regular people will lose healthcare coverage, Social Security, a healthy environment for the future. It's a clear trade.

Over the last decade, most of the wealth gains have gone to the very top. Yet, the so-called 1% and their supporters want to reduce Medicare and Social Security and Medicaid and throw people off their health insurance by the tens of millions. They expect to reduce, disrupt or eliminate many other sources of safety for people, as well, including the Women, Infants and Children program (WIC), which provides formula for poor babies and is slated for elimination or drastic reduction. In return, the very rich get a 3% cut in their taxes. Why are they so excited about these tax cuts, which they and their friends don't need, knowing that the consequences for many people will be dire?

First, if our unusual suspects were going to take resources from people who need them and give them to people who don't—à la tax cuts—having a way to conceal that intent would be handy. Our unusual suspects have come up with some stealthy strategies to accomplish those unpopular and distasteful goals. Here is just one: Assign the label *takers* to people who benefit from government assistance and refer to others—the 1%, for example—as *makers*. That sounds interesting. But what does that really mean?

According to the 'takers and makers' frame, the people at the top of the heap are the makers. They create jobs and wealth while others, the people on the bottom of the heap (takers), just spend money created by the makers—which they have not earned—in foolish or unnecessary ways. As the story goes, a man used food stamps to buy lobster. That example was broadcast widely by the abusive media and politicians and was used to show that the takers simply take too much and, worse, they take it from the makers. He got lobster! And he didn't even work for it! And that's wrong! Why should makers have to pay for a taker's lobster?

Think about just how degrading and demoralizing it is to people when they are told that they aren't worth health care or having enough food or going to college and that that if they are not well-off, it's their own fault. Who wants to be a *taker*? It's a vile term and they know it.

Stories like the that of the lobster and Jennifer's dollar store purchases serve a second objective for our abusers: they get us to fight with each other about who is getting more and whether that more is deserved. By limiting resources, we are forced to ask, *is that person really sick enough to be on disability or are they just lazy? Why don't I get food stamps when I work and she doesn't? Why does he get a pension and I don't?* We attack each other and begrudge one another our meager dollar-store purchases while the big guys make off with all of the real loot and are never asked to account for any of it.

The Trump Administration's budget, as proposed in 2017, cuts Meals on Wheels and after-school programs, the latter of which provides children from low-income families with two meals per day. How did they explain those cruel, seemingly senseless cuts? Like with the ACA, they claimed that they didn't work! Taxpayers, said the budget director, such as coal miners in West Virginia and single mothers in Michigan, shouldn't be asked to pay for programs that have no evidence of effectiveness.[29]

According to the Office of Management and Budget, those expenditures were wasteful, just like the man who ate lobster when he could have had chickpeas and just like Jennifer who buys three little figurines from the Family Dollar when one would suffice.

What is spent on programs like Meals on Wheels is comparatively little. Like Jennifer's dollar store purchases, they don't add up to much, but they become a powerful justification for the selfish who aim for total control. Jerry questions Jennifer's purchases; she does not question his. The unusual suspects in our political leadership question our purchases, like health care and electricity bills; we don't question theirs. They limit resources to weaken and diminish their victims and justify it by claiming wastefulness. Meanwhile, they achieve their ends—they get to keep 'their' money—while everyone else contributes to and funds their lifestyle with little choice.

The upward distribution of wealth is much more common than a trickle down. When Progressives started calling out the actual redistribution of wealth, Republicans accused them of inciting class war, but as wealthy businessman Warren Buffet retorted, "There's class warfare all right, but it's my class, the rich class, that's making war and we are winning."[30]

By claiming class war, our suspects imply that we, not them, started it by criticizing them or standing up for ourselves and that we are all on equal footing when it's actually not the same at all. Yes, she threw a shoe, but he landed her in intensive care. One single mother gets formula for her baby and the wealthy get tax cuts in the trillions. No, it's not the same.

While the makers buy boats or four-wheelers and enjoy nice cars and luxury vacations, believing that they deserve those things, those with a few bucks each week in food stamps are accused of over-spending or having things that are overly luxurious, like lobster. Not only are the takers supposedly over-spending, but they are held responsible for all financial problems.

It's not a tax policy making the rich richer that's the problem, it's the Social Security and health care that people rely on. Those entitlements are positively breaking the bank. It isn't gambling or partying or fun on a four-wheeler that causes Jerry's family debt. No, it's the three-dollar purchases each week. By keeping Jennifer's purchases in the forefront, less attention is paid to Jerry's excessive spending, allowing him to do whatever he wants without being held accountable.

The king is a deadbeat

The 'I'm King of the Castle' mentality, even though it seems archaic, still exists in lots of abusers' homes. Yet, many of these kings fail to provide adequate financial support for their progeny. They fail to pay what they owe because they believe that they shouldn't have to. It's their money, they made it and they darn well intend to keep it. Neither their partners nor the government can tell them what to do with their money.

We know what we call people who don't meet their obligations to their children. People who don't financially support those in their care, who don't help pay for food or school clothes or supplies or medicine are called *deadbeats*. I think the term is apt when referring to the unusual suspects, too. The reckless spending by the abusive wing of our political leadership does not give them permission to not make good for the people who count on them and to whom they have made promises.

On top of all that, the justification of 'we can't afford it,' is usually paired with a complementary justification that *even if we could afford it, you don't deserve it*. These are simply justifications that disguise the self-centered choices that abusers make.

It's hard to justify that you, as a lawmaker, chose a policy option that took away safety nets from single mothers or poor children or old people. *That* would be a terrible thing to do and you would be held responsible. It's easier to offer a justification that deflects responsibility. It wouldn't be their fault if the government simply can't afford it or if they prove people don't deserve what they were getting. These justifications, while effective on their own, also have a secondary yet important purpose: They put us—the victims in this scenario—in a childish place, as if we are hearing from our parents that we can't afford a pool or a new puppy—we must show fiscal discipline—and that even if we could afford it, we haven't been doing our chores and so we shouldn't be rewarded with something nice. But the stakes are a lot higher than pools and puppies.

While choices are made to deny people basic lifesaving measures, an abusive leadership claims that it's just the natural outcome of not having enough money. The takers, we are told, don't understand that we *just can't afford it*. We can't afford to waste our money on Social Security or health care or child care or low-cost college or food stamps or programs to end violence against women. Meanwhile, they offer tax cuts to the wealthy. It's like Jerry always telling his wife and family that money is tight while spending extravagantly on himself, which is, of course, why money is tight in the first place.

In this case, we know that despite their statements to the contrary, money is not tight in our country and, therefore, their paternalistic message has to be carefully spun in order to get us to accept their claims. To listen to them, Meals on Wheels and breakfast at school for poor children are ruining the country and must be dealt with immediately!

It's only natural

Anat Shenker-Osorio, in her book *Don't Buy It: The Trouble with Talking Nonsense about the Economy*, explains how the Right has found a nifty way to talk about the economy—one that we all seem to have picked up—one that leads people to believe that whatever economic hardship they face, its their own fault. Under this narrative, the only way to fix the economy is through "belt tightening, budget slashing, and total capitulation to the whims of Wall Street and big business."[31]

Naturally, this narrative works well for conservatives. Her thesis is that we must fight back against this narrative. Far too many believe it, to the detriment of the majority. It's a perfectly stealthy justification that lays the blame for economic mishaps on people who are not in fact to blame.

She continues:

For conservatives ideologically opposed to regulation, taxes, public expenditure, and social programs in general, this is an ideal state of conceptual affairs. It helps keep the true causes of economic malfunction in the shadows.[32]

And we have already seen how our suspects like to hide.

Worse, the story they tell is that whatever happens in the economy is just natural and can't be helped. The economy is just being itself and doing what it wants to do, good or bad. According to Shenker-Osorio, that is a common but wholly mistaken idea that lots of people, right and left, have unwittingly bought into. She says:

> We have the tendency to refer to the economy as something natural, even divine. Too often this cons audiences into believing that the way things are now from serial bubbles to the financial collapse of recent years is lamentable but largely out of our hands.[33]

But of course, that is far from the truth.

According to Shenker-Osorio, we talk passively about how things happen in the economy. We use phrases like "the unemployment rate is rising" and those passive constructions imply that nobody is behind any of it—that things happen magically and without any help from an actual person or persons, "thus concealing the choices that are always being made."[34]

By allowing decisions to look like everything is out of their hands and in the hands of an 'economy'—a separate being or force that they can't control—leaders deflect blame. When they make it seem like these results are natural, a lot of misery is created for people who wind up feeling that their bad circumstances are just inevitable—*the way things are.* In fact, abusive leaders make choices between and among expenditures and between and among people all the time. It just serves them well to claim otherwise.

This tactic is a favorite among domestic abusers who are infamous for their euphemistic descriptions of their abusive behaviors. I would hear in every group at least one person say that "mistakes were made," conveniently leaving out who made them and why. The first step—arguably the most critical—in helping abusers change is to challenge those passive constructions. We want them to accept that *mistakes weren't just made.* Somebody made them and that somebody was him—the abuser. How can we ever expect him to rehabilitate himself if he didn't do anything in the first place? If he didn't mean to do it, he can't very well prevent it from happening again.

When we realize that what happens in and to the economy—and in other policy areas for that matter—is also a choice, a political choice, made by people who have the power in our society, everything becomes a lot clearer. The truth is that choices are always made between possible courses of action. Giving tax cuts to wealthy corporations while cutting benefits like health care and Social Security, for example, is a choice even as some try to deny it. Claiming to have had no choice because that's just *how things are*, when making such decisions is no different than the abuser who says that his wife just flew out the door and landed on the sidewalk for some reason that is not clear to him. He and they are not in denial—they are denying. And there's a big difference between the two.

The tactics used by our usual suspects to gain power and control at home are no different from those employed by the big guys. They play the victim by claiming the poor are trying to steal from the rich and it isn't fair. They turn the tables by claiming we are inciting class war by wanting to redistribute wealth. They degrade and dehumanize by claiming we aren't worth even a few scraps. They use stealth by hiding information and preventing people from understanding what's really happening. They keep us off balance by reducing resources and forcing us to focus more on survival than on what's right. They rescue us from problems they created themselves and blame us, the victims, for all of the nation's financial problems. And if that's not enough, they divide and conquer by forcing us to fight over scraps. All of these tactics are carefully designed to further the agenda of the abuser. But we see them for what they are. Allow me to say again: Exposure is the key.

Now that we have seen what abusers do—how they behave—it would be reasonable to find out why they do those things in the first place. What's behind it all? What motivates them? What do they believe and how do their beliefs result in the use of tactics like these? How does it all fit together?

Shaping a woman

Pete was taught by his father (who was taught by his father) how to *shape a woman*. By that, his father meant that women must be taught to know their places and to never object or argue—a kind of brainwashing—so that after a while there is no need to inflict violence— the woman will comply voluntarily. It is a chilling, if sophisticated use of psychology. Pete described it this way:

> You start by building her up and making her feel like she's special and that you've never known anyone like her before. Then you start to withhold your praise and criticize her. She wants your favor and so she starts trying anything she can think of. When she starts acting in ways that you want and agreeing with you no matter what, you praise her. She'll get the idea of what you want. And you can control her completely.

Being shaped means that we put *ourselves in our own places* which makes life simpler for those who want us to just stay out of the way.

Sal's story

Another way for an abusive person to ensure compliance in those whom he wishes to dominate is to act abusively in random ways without warning. A man in one of my groups, Sal, said that his father would often wait until all of the family was seated around the table for dinner and then suddenly, randomly, and with no provocation, slap their mother or otherwise create some kind of scary scene. He said that they, the kids, always wondered why his father did that, but they assumed that their mother had done something wrong. She *must* have. Why else would their father have slapped her? It couldn't have been for *no* reason at all, right?

The real explanation, too sinister for young children to comprehend, was that Sal's father, like Pete, was performing his own version of shaping. He did it in order to prevent any future "uppityness" on her part. He did it to keep her in line. And the kids blamed her, blamed the victim, and sided with him because only a person who acts badly would get slapped at the dinner table in front of everyone, right?

Many victims are vigilant to the moods of others. They pay close attention to the facial expressions and non-verbals of people who have some power over them because it is a very hard place to be to not know what's coming next. In order to protect themselves, they must be prepared to take evasive action if necessary, and that's a well-reasoned survival strategy. But such vigilance eclipses a person's life in every way. Maintaining a state of vigilance takes a serious toll on a person's wellbeing. Having to be on guard all the time is exhausting, emotionally draining and seriously damaging. Lies and propaganda, assaults on our sense of reality and a lack of accountability in our leaders, who just keep getting away with it, is debilitating.

By being unpredictable, abusers keep people in a heightened state of expectation and anxiety, never knowing when something bad is coming.

It's like a haunted house where we are just moving through, anxiously awaiting the next scary thing to pop up. It's made all the worse because even though we know something is coming, we don't know when it will come or in what form. Imagine if the haunted house ride was never over—it'd be scary and nerve wracking. **Our leadership—the unusual suspects—like their counterparts, have built a haunted house just for us.**

Chapter 4

Controlling Forces

*Anger is anger whether provoked by a rebellious child
or a rebellious colony; hate is hate whether evoked by
an abusive spouse or a ruthless dictator.*

— Aaron T. Beck

In order to understand abusiveness, we need to understand abusers. Specifically, what do they want, anyhow? What motivates them? When they behave abusively, what are they trying to achieve? What are the commonalities between the usual and unusual suspects? In answering these questions, we are one step closer to finding a solution—especially when it comes to our abusive public figures and politicians. We have seen how they do it. Now we turn to the question of why.

Why they do it

In my experience working with abusers, there are three general classes of motives that can be inferred from their abusive behavior. The first, and arguably most important, is their dogged pursuit of power and control. The mother of all motives, I could count on one hand the number of abusers for whom this power motive was *not* the main one.

Next, we know that fear creates a motivation for abusive behavior; in fact, some of the worst atrocities in the history

85

of the world were, in essence, protracted reactions to fear. Fear of losing something, fear of being hurt themselves, and fear of seeming or actually being weak are all motivations for abuse.

Finally, there are those for whom demonstrating their power and dominance, even cruelly, is just for fun. Believe it or not, there are people who simply *like* being abusive and dominant.

There is always a reason

Many of us are tempted to view what abusers do as irrational, chaotic and unrestrained and we often explain terrible behavior just that way. We say that someone was out of control or that the person just *snapped*. We imagine that they have a bad temper and are just too impulsive to control themselves. But mostly, in fact, underlying the apparent chaos and irrationality of abusive behavior lies a coherent belief system with a clear objective. *There is always a reason.*

All people operate according to a set of rules, rationales and beliefs that motivate behavior. For some, these are their religious beliefs and guidelines, for others, they are the lessons ingrained by their parents or the culture in which they were raised. They might not be sensible. They might be harmful or dangerous. They might be grossly self-defeating. They might even result in total chaos. But there is nonetheless a pattern, a point and an underlying order to what we do most of the time. This seems a simple concept, but it's one we often overlook.

Violence and abuse no doubt have many causes beyond what I have suggested here. And someday we may understand them all. Until then, we can safely claim that people do what they do for a reason and abusive behavior is always motivated by something. No one does anything for no reason at all. We should always wonder about the motivations underlying abusive behavior and we will do so here in this chapter. What *are* these controlling forces that drive abusive behavior and how can we stop them?

The power motive

How we view our own and others' power largely determines how we will behave when we have it and when we don't. Most abuse, at least according to the abusers in my program who commit it, is perpetrated for the purposes of gaining or maintaining power. A lot of abusive men come right out and say that. And because violence is so closely associated with the concept, *power* in general gets a bad rap. But power itself is neither bad nor the cause of violence. There is nothing inherently wrong with wanting to have power—it isn't pathological. Powerful people often get more done and make bigger contributions to society. They usually feel better about themselves and others. So, what causes violence is not power itself but a *misunderstanding* of power—a perverse and wrong-headed view about what it is, why we want it, how to get it and what's required to hang onto it.

We might think that once people have a lot of power they need not *get more*; that there is a point at which we have enough and don't need anything additional. The same has been said about wealth. When you have enough money, you simply have enough. Who needs two yachts, right? But in reality, people always seem to want more of both. More power. More yachts.

In fact, power is so desirable and yet so elusive and fleeting, that people who hold a lot of it by most anybody's standards still feel that they don't have enough. When it comes to power and wealth, the insatiable need to get more can become the basis for abusive beliefs and behaviors. In other words, a sense of powerlessness—or the fear of becoming powerless—pervades the abusive worldview and leads to actions that are designed to protect that power at all costs.

Psychologists and philosophers have long theorized that violence is the product of perceived or actual powerlessness. Feelings of powerlessness are known to have been precursors to violence throughout history as individuals try to increase their sense of control and self-esteem through domination and force.[35]

Existential psychologist Rollo May, among others, believes that feeling powerless is the underlying and primary source of nearly all violence throughout history—the worst atrocities committed by those with a chip on their shoulder, people with something to prove who sought relief from the feeling of powerlessness.[36] What these individuals—the ones feeling powerless and seeking it out at all cost—don't understand, though, is that nobody can ever actually achieve true, unchallenged power and control. There is no such fix. No matter what the abuser does, success is not permanent because his brutal, self-created Darwinian jungle of a world is merciless and top status is always up for grabs. The abusive man's hold on his power is nothing if not fragile.

Furthermore, the people he tries to control usually resist. They stand up and fight. They get mad. They make it difficult for him. And even though the abusive man might control another's actions temporarily, he will never truly control what they think or how they feel. In the end, his control is all hat, no cattle—he scrambles incessantly to flex his pretend power, hoping one day he might actually have enough. What he continually seeks, but of course rarely finds, is total control.

The political struggle

Nowhere is this struggle more evident and more all-consuming than in the sphere of politics. Winning is the end-all in every case. Having total control is always the goal. It's a contest that causes tunnel vision and places power and dominance as the preeminent values. Unfortunately for those who believe in winning at all costs, they discover that being the winner does not and cannot last forever. Even worse for all of us, our needs and interests fall by the wayside, cast off by the strong, all-consuming need to prevail. We are a mere afterthought to the cause of winning it all. For our unusual suspects, winning, domination and total control matter most. Surviving the next election is *the* goal. Clearly, they believe it. Otherwise, they would not allow our country to collapse around us in order to preserve their powerful positions.

Fear

It's pretty much common knowledge that abusive men are sometimes violent out of fear. They believe that violence is necessary to defend against some possible hurt, betrayal, abandonment or rejection that may be coming their way. For them, paying close attention and being vigilant is a sensible but regrettable response to their expectation that people will hurt them sooner or later. They have rigid expectations for how people should behave and how things ought to happen—they prefer black and white; flexibility and shades of gray aren't really their forte. And these are similar traits we see leading to conservatism.

In late 2002, researchers at the University of Maryland published a widely read and frequently quoted meta-analysis on political conservatism. Specifically, they reviewed hundreds of studies on the topic over many decades and tested a theory they called *motivated social cognition*. The theory is that people adopt beliefs as psychological adaptations; in other words, they believe what they believe because they are motivated by something to do so. In this case, the study showed that what motivated political conservatism was mainly anxiety and fear.[37]

According to these researchers, the fears that motivate conservative ideology show up as resistance to change and an endorsement of inequality. So, when conservative ideologues express a dislike of any change in the status quo or seem to support various ongoing inequalities and discrimination, it may come from fear—fear of losing what they have, fear of catching what someone else has, fear of the unknown. No matter the reason, it seems that fear may be one source of political conservatism.

Other traits the study found to be associated with the conservative ideology that are motivated by fear include an intolerance of ambiguity (or wanting everything to have only one clear meaning), black-and-white simplistic thinking (as George Bush once said, "I don't nuance"), a need for closure or getting things done with, and a tendency towards aggression and revenge.[38] What does fear have to do with an endorsement of inequality and these other traits? Although we address support for inequality in both our usual and unusual suspects in the next chapter, it bears some explanation here.

First, conservatism is (or was) associated with wanting things to be the same, just by definition. People who are motivated by fear naturally want things to stay the same. Same is predictable; different is scary. Moreover, the way things used to be was good for people who had a lot and pretty bad for the people who didn't. Why would the haves (politically, socially, economically) want a change in such an arrangement? Domestic abusers need homes that are unequal in order to maintain their power. Our unusual suspects need that too, and for the same reasons. They need inequality in order to be powerful by comparison.

Intolerance for ambiguity—or wanting everything to have one answer—is also a protective mechanism. It's easier to just *know* what's right than to *wonder* what's right. Ambiguity and uncertainty? That produces anxiety. And when the world feels dangerous and people are afraid, aggression as a defensive strategy seems an understandable if not regrettable response.

It is not hard to imagine how this collection of beliefs and motives might lead to bad outcomes. When fear eclipses reflection—when inequality is never examined for its causes or consequence, when certainty crowds out analysis—anger, aggression and abusive behavior may result. This study helps us understand how political beliefs come about—how our feelings, such as fear, motivate our beliefs. But here's the main takeaway—its an *explanation*, not an excuse.

We have seen that fear and the desire for power—to *get more*—drive abusive behavior. Let's now look at one more, albeit upsetting, motivation for abusive behavior—abuse and violence just for fun.

For fun

Abusers tell us that there is something satisfying about successfully wielding power and, although fun may not be the exact right word, the point is clear that winning and wielding power and dominance—in lots of arenas, from sports to politics to the military and beyond—can be absolutely exhilarating. It may not seem obvious or even believable to say that playing out the abusive worldview can make for a good time. But for some, the use of power is quite satisfying and the word *fun* doesn't seem so outlandish. Throughout millennia, people have gone in droves to violent movies, sporting events, and to the Colosseum just to see people fight, get mutilated and even die. Nothing attracted a crowd like a public hanging or a witch burning.

Why do they go? Because it's entertaining, maybe it's even fun. If we consider what has come to be known as a "Trump Rally," we find ample evidence of the fun that comes from abusing opponents—including protesters and the press. Arguably, a good part of the popularity of the then-candidate came from his encouragement of abuse and violence, which the crowds ate up. He even said that back in the good ol' days, those who protested would have been "carried out on a stretcher."[39] He went so far as to volunteer to pay the legal expenses of anyone who got arrested for assaulting one.

Some years ago, at a town hall meeting as a part of Ron Paul's Presidential campaign, a discussion about health care featured crowds chanting loudly and enthusiastically, "*Let him die!*" when asked what should happen to an uninsured person with a terminal disease.[40] And let's not forget the hundreds of TV and radio and Internet personalities, like Bill O'Reilly, our specialist in 'abuse as entertainment,' who insult and bully people for the masses. Clearly, some people are just attracted to violence.

It's easy enough for us to label these people sadists—we try to explain and write off their heinous behavior as deviant, aberrant, or rare. But many, perhaps most, who commit acts of abuse and violence are not psychologically disturbed; their violence does not arise exclusively or predominantly out of pathology. If it did, we'd have to conclude that many millions of violent people committing a hideous assortment of brutal, violent acts over the centuries were as crazy as loons. Some were—lots were not. The abusive worldview makes plenty of room for people who act abusively and use violence for fun.

Power is political

We are sometimes lured into thinking that violence must be one of two types. In one case, we imagine that abuse and violence are committed for instrumental purposes— used for the purpose of achieving some goal. The second type might be thought of as the result of mental illness or a personality problem or emotional in origin, such as jealous rage. We think of it as reactive, hotheaded or impulsive. But this binary construction—instrumental or emotional— leads us astray.

I once heard political pundits try to explain abusive behavior by several of our unusual suspects as either psychological or political in motive, as if they required a different understanding. If a particular abusive act is done deliberately for some gain, it is therefore viewed as *political*. Of course, sometimes people react angrily to something and get themselves into trouble because of seemingly hotheaded or emotionally impulsive acts. But to the extent that abuse, as we have described it here, is a set of behaviors designed and delivered for the purposes of getting more power, then whether someone is psychologically "off," angry or upset is irrelevant. Whether someone acts without appropriate restraint is merely tangential to the underlying cause and reason.

Whether violence is instrumental—a consciously chosen strategy to get or avoid something—or more emotional and reactive in nature, the decision to hurt or abuse someone is, in the end, almost always a choice. It's always, in some sense, a *political act* and that concept blurs, and maybe obliterates entirely, the boundaries between the abuse inflicted on people for so-called political reasons and the abuse that our usual suspects inflict on their families to get the upper hand. In the end, and upon closer reflection, it's all about power and it's all political. But while we have now focused on the motives of abusers, we must remember that motives and beliefs operate in tandem.

Beliefs

> *On the whole, the right wing is attempting to impose a Strict Father ideology on America and, ultimately, the rest of the world.*
>
> — George Lakoff

Now I don't pretend to know exactly why any one person is violent. If I knew that, I'd have already been on more talk shows than Dr. Phil. I don't know whether there is something biological at work in our apparent attraction to violence, but it doesn't so much matter. Except for a few cases in which a person is so screwed up and delusional that a belief is unidentifiable or otherwise irrelevant, most of the men I work with hold beliefs that, in some way, permit and justify their behavior. Our work is about helping them understand

and remove those permissions. We help them see how their beliefs about the world frame what they do in it.

Some of these beliefs include:

- It's dominate or be dominated.

- The world is dangerous—survival is the most important consideration.

- I have to win at the game.

- It's every man for himself.

- Violence is normal, natural, and inevitable and there is no point in trying to change that.

- There is a natural and correct order: man over woman, over animals, over children, and over the environment. It is the strong over the weak.

- People who get hurt get what they deserve—except himself, of course; he never deserves his treatment. (He holds a double standard.)

- People should respect hierarchy and strict lines of authority.

- People in charge should not be questioned.

- People need to be put in their place and reminded to stay there. In general, men should be in charge.

- Winning is the thing—it's the only thing.

- Might is right; force is the universal language.

- My needs matter most.

◆ I am superior. (Rarely spoken, often implied.)

◆ It's my way or the highway.

◆ I deserve the good stuff that I get; I do not deserve anything bad.

◆ If I have it, it's because I deserve it—I am entitled.

◆ Inequality is normal.

◆ What is right is what I can get away with. Nothing bad will happen to me. (Often, unfortunately true.)

◆ I don't have to answer to anybody.

It's a jungle out there

Not every man holds every one of these beliefs, however. Some may hold several, while others may not exactly fit into any at all. With that said, after many years of working with abusive men, I have heard each of them time and again. I know them by heart. While I could get into a discussion of each and every one of these beliefs, it will serve our purpose better to focus on just a few: the belief that the world is dangerous, the belief that the abuser is in some way special, and the belief that they are—or have to be—at the top of the hierarchy. This list of beliefs provides a useful way to analyze our unusual suspects, too. There are—and will be— countless examples of abusive beliefs which apply easily and directly to them.

Some abusers believe quite sincerely that the world is dangerous and a place to be feared. It's a place where force is the most sensible response to threats that lurk everywhere and where only the strong survive. In fact, it's a jungle out there. Of course, if it's a jungle, *survival* becomes job one.

Everybody is out for himself and because it's all a contest, the abuser concludes that he had better be on his game. He imagines that in order to survive, he must be tougher than the other guy because weakness makes him a vulnerable target.

In the jungle, there are predators and there is prey—one must use stealth and be bigger or smarter or faster to come out as the predator and not as the prey. Vigilant scanning of the environment for threats is naturally required. And as for trust? Well, that has no meaning at all. To trust would be naïve, silly and unwise. This jungle world is an ultra-competitive place with winners and losers and that's just *the way things are.*

I am special and above the rules

When it comes to beliefs that contribute to abusive behavior, one of the biggest is the belief that the abusers are, in some way, special. This gives them permission to act however they want and do whatever they want to do to get whatever it is they want.

More than a few of the people I've worked with believe that they are special and, therefore, entitled to do as they please. Convinced that ordinary rules don't apply to them, they expect to get away with bad behavior. They think they can slide by, talk their way out, skirt the edges and not get caught or be held to account. This makes it okay to lie to, degrade and assault the people around them and hold their partners to a double standard.

When one is exceptional, the rules don't apply to them, but they still do apply to everyone else. In this worldview, getting what you can for yourself is what matters most and self-centeredness is perfectly appropriate and justifiable—that's how the game goes. If you step on somebody, well, it's nothing personal; they should have been paying more attention. The ends always justify the means, however unsavory. And of course, they decide which ends matter and which means are justified.

Top dogs and strict fathers

If nothing else, the abusive worldview is strictly hierarchical—a place where some are naturally superior to others. Adults are superior to children and animals; men are superior to women; whites are superior to blacks and other minorities, and so on. Such belief in one's essential superiority makes it easy to justify bad treatment of those who are different or who have less power and status. And it provides a handy justification for bad and selfish behavior.

With domestic abusers, this mentality allows them to treat the people around them—their wives and children—like lesser beings. They can exert their dominance over them in multiple ways without concern for whether or not that is acceptable. To them, they are top dog and it's their right to treat others however they want. When it comes to those in the public eye, particularly in politics, this same view allows similar behaviors. They exert their dominance over others, particularly minorities, without concern for whether it is right or acceptable to do so.

Linguist George Lakoff, in his book *Moral Politics*, suggests that in this dominance hierarchy, the moral arrangement embraced by conservatives is as follows:[41]

1. God has dominance over human beings.

2. Human beings have dominance over nature.

3. Adults have dominance over children.

4. Men have dominance over women.

Where you are in the hierarchy naturally effects what you get to do and to whom. The use of tactics of power and control become necessary for those at the top to maintain their place. For purveyors of the abusive worldview, this hierarchy is natural, moral, and perfectly justified, so it's important to punish those who attempt to undermine it or subvert it. For example, people like environmentalists and animal rights activists violate rule 2; parents, parenting experts and child welfare activists violate rule 3; feminists violate rule 4; and, of course, anyone who's not Christian and doesn't strictly adhere to Christian precepts or is not in favor of renovating the US according to biblical law violates rule 1. All of these people need to be straightened out so that the ones who deserve to be at the top can stay there without interference. Sticking to these hierarchies and forcing their families to maintain them as well is key to the Strict Father's control of his household and to the orderliness of the country, and in fact, the world.

Lakoff's Strict Father paradigm is everywhere in domestic violence. In this view, a good parent will teach their child that the world is a harsh place—a jungle, unforgiving and competitive. He'll explain that survival is possible only through cunning, brute strength, a show of power and subsequent garnering of respect to deter threats. The Strict Father knows that his kids can't be weak, or else.[42]

He thinks, "What kind of parent would I be if I allowed my children to actually believe that the world is safe?" Therefore, when he deprives them of love, affection or nurturing, it is for their own good. Punishment and control are part of the training required to live in the jungle and build the character necessary to make it out there. If he, as the father, makes life hard, well, at least when they get out into the world, they won't be surprised. This is one way, as we have seen, in which the abusive worldview is spread from generation to generation.[43]

There are always people who just won't stay in line or give our suspects—the Strict Fathers—the respect they think they deserve. What to do? How can people be controlled who would just as soon not be? Several options present themselves to the would-be Strict Father, though they are by no means the only ones. The first is to use force. That is definitely effective, but not preferred because it looks really bad and things might get out of hand or go wrong. The second is to fool people—and convince them to go along voluntarily—into seeing that controlling them is for *their own good.* If one can get people to see things that way, then perhaps they will go along more often than they would have if they thought you were controlling them for *your good.* We can see how this works. If you can convince people that your self-interest is actually *their* self-interest, whether it really is or isn't, then you will have fewer challenges to your rule. A number of examples probably come to mind.

Unfortunately, the concept of the Strict Father is one that people believe in. It's a frame that people *get.* They believe that being strict and having high standards and promoting strong will and resilience in children is good for them— it's just that the Strict Father idea doesn't work like people think.

People who are raised in strict and abusive homes and who are taught that the world is a harsh place where they had better buck up, do not become happier or more resilient or more powerful. They become the opposite.

The Strict Father story is hard to challenge because it's been popular for quite some time, but it needs to be exposed for the actual harm it causes. If we persist in advertising this abusive mentality, furthering the idea that punishment is good and moral, that submission by women and children is desirable and even necessary, then we will have to admit that we're embracing it not for its results, which are clearly bad, but for the ideology that attaches to it. And whose interests are being served when an abusive worldview is allowed to reign when it's passed down like a family heirloom?

Psychologist Stephen Ducat, in his book *The Wimp Factor*, explores research that has found that men who grow up in violent homes or where discipline was harsh were much more likely to adopt a conservative belief system, scoring higher on measures of authoritarianism. Those who experienced harsh discipline as children were more likely as adults to favor a government or party that maintained that disciplinary worldview. These men wanted leaders who, like their fathers, kicked ass, defended the country's honor, valued aggression and revenge and went to war easily. They also scored higher on measures of misogyny and homophobia. In other words, having been treated badly as a child resulted in a conservative or right-wing ideology—an abusive worldview—more often than a liberal one.[44]

Sadly, we in the US today apparently accept a view in which Dad beats up the neighbor. Dad tells the kids—just as the government tells the citizens—that they are better, superior and tougher and that they ought not to take any crap from anybody. That worldview says to "get back out there and kill that guy" for being disrespectful.

This is what the abusive worldview teaches about power:

+ Someone must be in charge.

+ Powerful positions are natural.

+ It's dominate or be dominated.

+ Power can be best achieved through force.

+ There is only so much to go around.

That doesn't leave much wriggle room, for sure. When we ask ourselves why some abusers are so focused on danger, so vigilant to threats and so prepared to eviscerate anyone who get in the way, it might be because they grew up in Strict Father (read: abusive) households and they learned the lessons inherent in it.

It may seem an obvious point that we act on the basis of our beliefs and that, if we want change in some aspect of our lives, we can often accomplish that shift by changing how we think. But for all its obviousness, it gets missed most of the time. So accustomed are we to thinking of our beliefs as something more—as the truth—that we rarely think to challenge any of them. We know that these beliefs, the ones that float freely around in the abusive worldview, are dangerous and lead to bad decisions, abuse and violence. That's why unearthing and reflecting on them can't wait.

Now that we understand better why abusers behave as they do—what motivates them—and the abusive beliefs to which they adhere, we turn our attention to how those beliefs and behaviors affect those who live under and around them.

Self-Esteem

I have often been asked about how self-esteem relates to abusiveness. Is high or low self-esteem the culprit? That's a good question. Many abusers act as if they think highly of themselves. They conduct themselves as though they are special and entitled and above the rules. But is that how they really feel? Aren't most bullies insecure, down deep, and isn't that why they constantly have to prove themselves?

I have seen plenty of abusers whose insecurities masquerade as bravado and arrogance, but I have also seen those who really do believe, both on the surface and down deep, that they are quite special. They aren't insecure—they are self-important and if you challenge their importance and entitlement in any manner or appear to treat them with less respect than they believe they deserve, they can become angry, blaming, vindictive and even dangerous.

Neither insecurity nor narcissistic entitlement fully explains abusiveness. Powerful or powerless, superior or inferior, it's not always easy to tell which feeling is in charge. It would be a mistake to assume that all abusers feel badly about themselves or that entitlement disguises low self-esteem and insecurity. Sometimes it might, but not always.

Those with a lot—those high on the economic ladder and those who have been spoiled into thinking mostly about themselves and less about others—may grow up to lack empathy for people with less. Some may recall the teenager who was diagnosed in the press as being afflicted with 'affluenza' because his sense of entitlement was used as a justification for his lack of empathy and abusive behavior. The argument was that he was so entitled that he just didn't know any better.

However, children exposed to violence and poverty—those in no way treated as special or entitled, who are more likely to have been victims—may also grow up to lack empathy.

Both those with everything and those with nothing are susceptible to not caring much about other people. Therefore, the more our world develops both a small group with a lot and a large group with a little, the more our values of compassion and empathy will be widely threatened.

Chapter 5

The Fallout of Inequality and Abuse

By changing nothing, nothing changes.

—Tony Robbins

The fallout of abusive behaviors, whether they occur in an abusive home or at the level of culture, are much the same. In this chapter, we review some but not all of those effects and will focus on how inequality, in particular, creates and perpetuates serious conditions in both places. The good news—*there is good news*—is that by reducing inequality and empowering more people, we can reduce or prevent many of these terrible effects.

Of course, the abuser's home may again be instructive as we consider how that might happen. It is common knowledge that exposure to violence and abuse is disastrous; it has serious and often long-term consequences that have been identified in a multitude of places. They include but are definitely not limited to the following:

+ Depression
+ Poverty
+ Crime
+ Lack of education and unemployment

- Substance abuse
- Homelessness
- Major illness
- Shortened lifespan
- Loss of trust
- Hopelessness
- Fear
- Anger
- Lowered self-esteem
- Inability to manage emotions
- Broken families
- Loss of civility
- Extreme financial cost
- Susceptibility to authoritarian influences
- Tendency to accept and normalize abusive behavior

These effects, which often last the course of a person's lifetime, begin early on as children struggle to live with and adapt to an abusive home.

Kaiser Permanente conducted a long-term study on the effects of adverse childhood experiences, known commonly as ACE.[45] They discovered that children who were exposed to physical, sexual or emotional abuse and neglect were more likely than their peers to grow up to suffer a multitude of serious problems such as cancer and heart disease. They didn't live as long either—their lifespans were an average of 20 *years* shorter than children who grew up without abuse and neglect.[46]

Research also showed that children exposed to violence are more likely to view the world as dangerous—because it has been—and that those kids have a harder time fighting off the devastating effects of poverty and are more likely to be anxious, lack resilience and be constantly vigilant to threats. Because they see the world as dangerous, they may, themselves, become dangerous. Some will come to lack both trust in and empathy for others.[47]

The effects of living under abuse are long-lasting and insidious. A person's view of the world is shaped by exposure to abuse. I have seen it time and time again. Abused people can't hold jobs, they get depressed, and they suffer from anxiety. They have a hard time getting along with others and just dealing with life in general. And then sometimes they become abusers themselves. They wind up homeless and addicted to drugs or alcohol. The real outcome is that a person's entire life is entirely abbreviated—if not literally, then in terms of it's quality.

Mary grew up in an abusive home but nobody would have ever suspected it. Her father was the nicest guy; I actually knew him and never in a million years would I have suspected him of anything even remotely abusive. Yet, he kept his family in a constant state of anxiety and fear, wondering when he was going to "blow" and cause a scene or ruin some event, like a vacation or family dinner. Mary had lots of health problems—she could barely walk without a cane. I used to wonder how she got that way and in my ignorance, I thought she could do something about it if she wanted to. I sort of blamed her for it. Of course, had I known then what I know now, my opinion about her problems would have been vastly different.

I've known others, too, who have lived in abusive homes and some that lived in very controlling environments with parents who dictated everything and didn't let them have much freedom in what they thought, said or did. Those people, too, were either obese or sick or eating disordered or emotionally unstable as they tried to find ways to assert some autonomy and control over their own lives. The effects can hardly be overstated, but we know that abuse is not destiny—people can recover and lead lives that are happy and productive. The problem is that we don't know about the abuse early enough, if ever, and so we can't intervene. Exposure, as I have already said, is curative.

Let's expand our view to see what an abusive culture and its carriers create. The following is a summary as we have already covered the fallout, in one form or another, in previous chapters.

Since the 2016 US Presidential campaign and the swearing in of President Trump, trust in our institutions such as courts, banks, corporations, Congress and the Oval office has evaporated. But in fact, that trust had been eroding for years. A horrific financial crisis in 2008, which led to the infamous bailouts of big banks and the tossing aside of everyone else, fundamentally changed the level of faith that people have in institutions. Trump accelerated it, true, but it had already begun.

In any case, we can't or don't believe anything we hear or read or see anymore and that total lack of trust is alienating, scary, and, therefore, psychologically harmful. The country is divided—red and blue—with little hope of making it better. People are afraid, angry and even aggressive. Many of my therapist friends tell me that they are overwhelmed by clients who are depressed and anxious and mad. The degradation of minority groups has increased, often with few consequences for those who commit crimes against them—and many people fear for their own wellbeing. Will they be deported? Pulled over for a missing taillight and shot? Gunned down in a shopping mall or kindergarten classroom? It's become a jungle out there, where everyone is left to fend for themselves. Everything has become a competitive hustle and everyone is a commodity. A few will win. *Most will lose.*

The hierarchy under which we now live is steep. The lack of opportunity and rampant inequality intrinsic to this system causes widespread, abject hopelessness. We are stewing in an ultra-competitive, anxious, winning-obsessed world where nobody ever actually feels like they have enough, including those that clearly *do* have enough. Our leadership is seemingly indifferent to the needs of many of their constituents and to their obligations to serve them. Many of those constituents feel that they and their needs don't matter to anyone. They certainly don't feel represented.

And why should they? They can see plain as day that their leaders would and do sacrifice their constituents' wellbeing in order to *get more* for themselves. The abusive worldview is circulating.

As we know, exposure to domestic violence increases the risk for major illnesses such as cancer, heart disease and stroke and contributes to rates of premature death. And now we know that overall levels of health are worse and life expectancy is lower in societies that are more unequal.[48] In fact, depression rates are higher in the US states with the highest levels of inequality—the more unequal the state, the higher the prevalence of depression.

Acceptance of authoritarianism is also present in unequal places. Just as domestic abusers who grew up in violent homes are likely to believe that authority deserves greater respect and that children should always be obedient, people living in unequal places also hold those beliefs.[49] And those beliefs, when present at the cultural level, endanger the vitality and wellbeing of our democratic institutions. When people look to authoritarians, believing that some people are entitled to rule over others, they are more likely to accept dictatorial leadership, so inequality is, in fact, a real threat to democracy. One notable finding is that the more time the right wing spends in office over time, the higher the general inequality.[50] As we have seen, the Strict Father mentality doesn't seem to produce anything good in either the short or long term.

And it's not just those who are directly affected that suffer these consequences. Research shows that just living in an unequal society is dangerous to your health, regardless of your own status.[51] Whether rich or poor, it is not possible for anyone to escape the ravages of pervasive and growing inequality. People may want to believe that what happens to victims stays with those victims, but of course that's not true. Domestic abuse spills over in many ways—and now we also realize that societal inequality affects all of us, advantaged and disadvantaged alike. Even those with a lot socially and economically suffer from the lower status of their fellow citizens. We are all in this together.

In 2016, Florida Governor Rick Scott made a statement to the press after a horrific mass shooting at the Orlando airport. In that statement, he wondered what could be done to stop such heinous acts in the future.[52] He seemed genuinely concerned and that made me think about how to answer him. Is there anything that can be done to limit the number of people who march into an airport, or anyplace else, and blow people away? Yes, I think there may be.

Without in any way excusing that killer, there are some ways that we can build a better place in which we all live. If I were giving advice to that Governor and people like him, I would say the following:

> First, Governor, you can stop treating people like they don't matter. That creates a sad, hopeless and even desperate culture. Give people health care, so they can get treatment of mental health and substance abuse and other life-threating diseases before they take extreme measures; if they already have that help,

113

don't threaten to take it away. Don't tell them they aren't good enough to warrant it. Don't celebrate your constituents' harm, like the Republican House did after passing their destructive healthcare bill. Ensure that people have basic security and that they live in safe neighborhoods and go to good schools.

Don't waste time looking for talking points to justify why you should add to your wealth at the expense of people who count on you. We've heard all of them before and they aren't fooling anyone. Getting a big tax cut might be kind of nice, but should it be at the expense of society as a whole?

Inequality perpetuates gross imbalances in power and opportunity and it makes things very much worse. If you want change, you and those like you could take steps to reduce inequality and provide people with basic security. You could do that and a lot more, but if you don't or won't, you and yours will inevitably be at risk, too.

Just living in places where inequality is great hurts everyone, whether you are at the top or at the bottom, inside the gate or outside of it. You aren't immune. You can live behind a gate or in a castle, that's true, but eventually, the kind of culture you create for others will be the one in which you and your family must also live.

Yes, we are all in this together.

Today, our unusual suspects have constructed a wall between themselves and the rest of us. They pretend not to hear us. Our problems don't affect them much and while it may seem to be working pretty well, like an abuser's home, it won't last. It never has.

Parallels between the effects of exposure to domestic violence and exposure to inequality are clear. Wherever inequality is allowed to increase, wherever power imbalances are ignored or left to grow, the consequences are potentially devastating for everyone. Turns out that abuse doesn't really pay after all.

Wouldn't it be reasonable then, to ask, *on what planet we would ever accept consequences like these? Is it possible that the self-interest and greed and power-mongering of an abuser are worth these costs? Would we actually accept these horrific problems in order to make sure that that no abuser ever has to confront his behavior or change?* That would be unimaginable and yet we make policy and engage in common practice as if that were true. The abuser gets every benefit of the doubt.

We allow and even promote the view in which inequality is an acceptable, if regrettable, state of affairs. We make it worse. But the reasons to pay attention to these behaviors and the worldview that supports them are enormous.

We could actually help children grow into happy and productive adults if we wanted to. We could reduce poverty, make sure kids aren't hungry, deal with domestic violence abusers and protect people from them, provide good schools near children's homes, reduce crime, provide health care including mental health and substance abuse treatment, and offer early childhood education and similar programs. These all work to reduce stress on families and help children become more resilient.

The worst part is that we know how to make it better. We know how to stop the spread of this abusive worldview—and we even have the power to do so. Halting growing inequality, the division between ultra-rich and the devastatingly poor, is one way. If we want a better world with less crime, less violence, less anger, and more hope, we need to minimize the gross inequality between us. Yet, rarely is that offered in popular discourse as either a cause of our problems or a cure for them. Our effort—meager as it is—to create security and safety for families is under threat.

Power imbalances lead to abuse

When we talk about preventing domestic violence, for example, reducing inequality in the relationship is rarely, if ever, offered as a solution despite the fact that we know an unequal power balance is a primary facilitator of abusive behavior. Instead, we talk about managing anger or improving communication or dealing with substance abuse. Likewise, when we ask how we can repair our broken country, we don't very often decide that we must reduce inequality and balance out the power between us. Rather, we conclude that the answer is to be nicer and stop calling people names—an idea I wholeheartedly support—but that alone will not fix anything.

Many of the most important effects of inequality on societies are nearly identical to those we associate with exposure to domestic violence. Lack of trust,[53] lower levels of altruism, less participation in civic life,[54] violent crime[55] and worse physical and mental health are just some of the outcomes of societal inequality.[56]

The Strict Father mentality, with its emphasis on hierarchy and inequality, leads to harm. Even men in a domestic abuser group can come to see that being beaten or threatened or terrified or kept in an inferior position is not the way to help children or a country become strong and happy. The Strict Father model is passé—it isn't the right model anymore, not that it ever was.

When abusers are allowed to get, keep and misuse power, while everyone else gets less, the hopelessness that attaches to inequality will never resolve. Dealing with unequal power and opportunity and promoting democratic processes where everyone matters and can be heard, whether in our homes or in our society, is likely the only answer. So, how can we ensure that our politicians are held to account for their abusive behavior? To answer that, we must turn to this important question: Is there any hope for these aficionados of power and control to change? And if so, what can we do to help them along in the process?

Chapter 6

Will They Change?

Wisdom consists of the anticipation of consequences.

—Norman Cousins

The usual suspects provide a lens through which we can view and understand abusiveness at higher levels. Examining how domestic abusers think and act and the effects of their behavior on the people around them have given us insight into others—public figures in particular—who also model this abusive worldview. We'll now take this one step further to explore if and how these abusers can change.

As we in domestic abuse work know, there are two common questions—ones we are asked over and over, by nearly every single domestic abuse victim we work with:

Q: Why do they act that way, so abusively?
A: Because they want to, it works, and they can.

Q: Will they ever change?
A: Not without a good reason and not if they don't have to.

When asked this last question—if he will ever change—the actual answer is that he might. Some do. But he has to want to change. He has to feel some pressure to do so. So long as he and his associates and friends and family and culture all make it seem like no big deal and so long as he gets his way and does not have to confront the damage he causes or how counterproductive his behavior is to his ultimate goals, then he won't change. There will be no motivation. In fact, all the motivation will be operating, as we have seen in preceding chapters, in the other direction. And he will likely get worse and not better.

Conditions for change

We know that in order for a domestic abuser—a usual suspect—to change, three conditions must be present: negative consequences for abusive behaviors, not rewards and applause; honest self-reflection, not denial and justification; and acceptance that abusive behavior is always a choice, regardless of the justifications manufactured to make it appear otherwise. It is only when each of these three factors is present that a domestic abuser has any hope of reducing and eliminating the violence in his home.

We have to accept that many, if not most, of the purveyors of this worldview, the usual and unusual among them, will not change of their own accord. The negative consequences for bad behavior are too light, too few and, sometimes, downright reinforcing. In fact, there is too much benefit and too much cultural support to warrant their changing anything without outside pressure.

Unaccountable power always grows worse—it escalates. Therefore, consequences are needed to regulate the behavior of powerful people. Abusers, especially, need limits on their behavior and consequences for actions that harm others. Not only that, but they require an ability to reflect on their behaviors. When abusive people change, it's because they become acutely aware of how their actions harmed others and, ultimately, even themselves. Finally, it may be natural to want to get more power, but abusiveness in the pursuit of it is not inevitable. It's a choice and that understanding—that we choose our behavior—is both a fundamental truth and a prerequisite for change.

Getting away with it

One of the primary factors in whether an abuser will change—likely the most important one—is whether or not he is held accountable for the actions he takes and whether or not he suffers any negative consequences. Unfortunately, it's all too common that abusers—whether our usual or unusual suspects—get away with their behavior. And getting away with it and change are definitely in opposition. Nothing more seriously interferes with the possibility of change than an abuser's recognition that he can do what he wants and that nobody will hold him to account.

There is a multitude of ways that abusers have discovered to *get away with it* and we reviewed some of those ways in previous chapters. The best way to *prevent* his *getting away with it* is to expose the tactics, beliefs, motives and explanations that he uses and to explore and name the true fallout. Abusers need to come face to face with the consequences of their abusive behavior.

We also need to stop applauding abusers for not doing worse. All too often, when an abuser does something that is reasonably acceptable, that is to say, when he does something that simply meets basic standards, he expects and often gets applause and congratulations. We reward him for not doing even more dangerous or destructive things. Donald Trump is a prime example of this tendency. When he read a speech and didn't make too many mistakes, he was applauded, heralded as finally Presidential. A lot of us know how to read a speech, but that doesn't make us Presidential, does it?

Over the past decade and beyond, we have seen how some powerful groups have gotten away with very bad behavior. They may have used their positions of leadership for personal profit, in violation of ethical standards, if not actual law. There are widespread allegations and news reports that Secretary of Health and Human Services, Tom Price, bought and sold stocks whose value he could control through his official position.[57] Another example is Scott Pruitt, head of the EPA, who by all accounts is secretive about his connections to the oil and gas industry and various billionaires and is currently being sued by the Center for Media and Democracy.[58]

The entire Trump enterprise appears to be profiting from his new role as leader of the free world. These guys and others like them may be using our money—taxpayer money—in furtherance of their personal aims and, at least so far, doing so without any consequence whatsoever. And of course, Donald Trump never released his tax returns so we can't know whether he has our interests or his own at heart, although many suspect it's the latter.

Forget about it

One effective way to avoid accountability is to implore people to just forget about any prior bad acts. *Let's move on*, we hear abusers say frequently. In our usual suspects, this is a standard suggestion. Abusers accuse their wives of having long memories. They don't appreciate their partners bringing up the past and remembering incidents of abuse and violence. And of course those abusers would like people to forget about it because then they will get to do it again. We all know the saying that those who forget the past are doomed to repeat it.

In 2017, the reality of the Russian attempt to take over our entire democracy began to sink in. And it was very scary. But what did Donald Trump say about it? He and his allies said, in essence, "Well, there are two sides." The Russians deny that they did it and, therefore, because it's just a he said/she said thing, we ought to forget about it. They used the words "move on" rather frequently, which I found chilling because I have heard it so many times before in my abuser counseling groups.[59] In other words, forget about it.

In fact, the very best predictor of future behavior is past behavior. If we allow abusive acts to be forgotten, if we just move on, every time will be like the first time and the abuser will have a clean record and a clean slate upon which to do it all the more.

As we watch our political leadership, many of us are disgusted by their lack of accountability. Crimes, lies, ethical violations at the highest levels, and worse go unchecked.

Nobody does anything about them. That's bad on its face, as there is no justice for their victims, but what makes it worse is that allowing abusers to get away with their abuse actually *worsens* their behavior. It almost never gets better. Why should it, after all, when they can see that nobody is going to hold them to account? If we want to change abusive behavior, we have to stop letting abusers get away without consequences.

Standing by

When bad acts are not acknowledged by anyone, the victims of those acts become disheartened. Victims say all the time that *nobody ever does anything to help*. Victims are left, not uncommonly, to fend for themselves while bad acts are excused over and over. Nicole Brown Simpson once asked why nobody ever did anything about her abusive husband, OJ. Good question.

So, another way in which abusers *get away with it* is that many people decide not to intervene. Victims often find themselves alone while friends and family and other more powerful forces either do nothing or take the side of the abuser. In domestic violence, we use the term *bystanders* to describe people who are witness, directly or metaphorically, to abuse and whom we expect to stand up for the victim. One of the saddest truths for professionals in domestic violence is that people often don't stand up for victims. They stand by, true enough, but they don't help.

What's even worse is that people who *could* hold bad actors to account, who have the power to do so, just don't. They stand by and do nothing but watch. Abusers and complacent bystanders do not a good society make. In what will become an iconic image, President Trump and the Republican House members—the vast majority of whom are white males—drank beer and celebrated in the White House Rose Garden the passage of a law that will surely harm many millions of people while providing a tax break to the wealthy. Many worry whether those actions will ever be truly exposed, whether those that made it happen will ever be held to account or, whether they will, in the end, just get away with it.

Why do people let it happen?

You might wonder why people go along with the abuser. Why are they complicit in his getting away with it? Can't they see what he has done? In fact, abusers and bullies get more support than do victims. Let's face it, nobody wants to be a victim but lots of people want to be powerful. Given a choice between being a bully and being a victim, many more people would choose the bully. People identify with powerful people and want to be like them—they don't aspire to being a victim very often. People want to be on winning teams, not losing ones. The exception to this principle, of course, is playing a victim in order to get more.

People also try to placate seemingly powerful people. Of course they would want to do so—it's *some* protection, after all. People worry that if they antagonize the bully, he will feel no guilt about or hesitation in taking revenge—and that is a correct assumption.

There is another more obvious reason playing out. Even though our entire democracy is arguably at risk because of Russian interference,[60] there is one political party—the Rebulicans—that seems willing to allow it to keep happening just so that they don't lose power. They can stop this, but they don't. This single-minded pursuit of power is the real problem as getting more eclipses everything else.

When I began writing this book, my hope was that we would learn as much about abusers from watching their infamous counterparts as we would learn about the abusive political leadership from reflecting on domestic abusers. Through the course of writing, one thing has become plain: If we want change in either, we must put them and those who support them under constant, unrelenting pressure. All of our suspects have been sliding by and getting away with bad behavior for years. Exploitative, unaccountable and immune to consequences, is it any wonder they have escalated their abusive leadership? Nobody ever really got in their way. But is that the way we think it should be? When did self-centeredness begin to look like a good model for everybody? Would we really want this to be the prevailing view and way forward for all of us? If we don't stand in their way now, will we ever?

Collapse is a consequence

Abusers' actions cause families to collapse. Of that there is little doubt. And if we can learn anything from what happens to people who live with an abuser, we will have to face that a full-scale collapse may be on the horizon. Jared Diamond, in his book *Collapse: How Societies Choose To Fail or Succeed*, tells us that societies fall apart when leaders become divorced from the consequences of their actions. In other words, consequences both drive and restrain our actions and teach us lessons about how we should act and what we can get away with.[61] But when consequences can be easily ignored and avoided, that distance leads to bad decisions and terrible outcomes.

Lots of people, no doubt accurately, describe the political leadership as being in the "Beltway bubble," removed from the real issues and problems of their constituents. For example, why do legislators ignore what the majority of us say we want? It's because they want to and they can. Through gerrymandering, many of these legislators have safe seats; they will never lose and so they don't have to be responsive to anyone but their small, gerrymandered districts. They are divorced from the consequences of their actions. And they are bought off, as we know, by donors with nefarious motives who are, likewise, well protected from the chaos they create. Without consequences, there is rarely any change.

Abusers make sure that they rarely suffer any consequence for their behavior, considering themselves exempt from rules that apply to others, so that they don't have to change. And ironically, because they don't change, their families eventually fall apart and abusers get the reverse of what they want. They lose everything. Karma is a concept of which our suspects need reminding.

Reflections on getting more

Once our suspect has experienced consequences and has some motivation to change, it's time for him to reflect on how he has behaved and to what ends. But about what should he reflect? In abuser groups, reflection usually includes, at minimum, a consideration as to whether his behavior has been productive for *him*. Is he really getting what he wanted? And of course, what are the effects on those he has harmed?

What are the beliefs that he has taken as the truth? For example, is the Strict Father model actually true? Is the world really a jungle where only the strong survive or is that just one belief of many? And is it true that his abusiveness was just natural? Was it out of his hands? Was it out of control behavior or was it a choice? How has he tried to explain it all away?

Now, just because an abuser sees his beliefs as *beliefs* and not the *truth*, doesn't guarantee change, but without such reflection, it makes it a whole lot harder. Honest reflection makes it difficult for an abuser to keep pretending that his actions have not been that big of a problem and that they are normal and acceptable behaviors.

It's not too late

The Texas Council on Family Violence conducted a focus group of domestic violence abusers. There were three key messages that moved abusers to think about change. The first message was that their children were suffering because of their abusive behaviors, a situation which many had tried to rationalize away in the past. The second was that help was available—that had never before occurred to many—and the third was that things didn't have to be the way that they were, which was a relief and source of hope.

Many of the abusers with whom I've worked absolutely believed that it was too late to undo the damage that they caused to their children. But I could counter, accurately, that their children were not necessarily damaged forever from the abuser's behavior. They were not beyond repair. In fact, when abuse stops and the abusive person apologizes and acknowledges that he was wrong, the negative effects of abuse on his children don't just halt—they can be reversed! That realization always provides enormous motivation. Changing will help. It's not too late! *It's never too late.*

Power: Let's think about it

We have come to understand that getting more power is the primary motive within the abusive worldview. It drives all else. Therefore, it behooves the abusers to reflect on it as well. What is it? Why does he want it? Is the appearance of power just as good as the real thing?

In fact, power, in the way that the abusive man thinks about it, can never be permanently attained since no sooner does he acquire it than does someone else comes along with the desire and ability to take it away. There will always be someone with more power. The abuser is, by logical extension, in a state of relative and continual powerlessness. When everything is dominated by black and white thinking, there are only the powerful and the powerless—the world becomes a very insecure and threatening place. It requires constant control. And it's exhausting.

In the case of our *usual* suspect, all that he wants and tries to get through his violence and control is lost; it's the ultimate self-defeating behavior. His wife trusts him less or not at all. His kids can't stand him or don't respect him. He is plagued by doubt and must be constantly on guard and vigilant to danger, creating, as he has, an environment which is, in fact, dangerous for him and others. He waits for people to hurt him and for the other shoe to drop.

When the domestic abuser reflects on his world of *powerful versus powerless*, he comes to realize that he will eventually end up powerless because no one gets to be *the* top dog forever. The abusive man's efforts to keep control of his partner works only in the short term and on the most superficial level because the majority of women who live with abusive men eventually leave them.

Just like a domestic abuser, our political leadership is not prone to reflection. Politics is tactical and often short-term. Politicians often focus on getting and keeping power for as long as possible, and it's not until they are forced to do so that they can or will reflect on the impact they are having on the people they represent.

We can imagine that our leaders don't stop to think about whether the country will really benefit from tax cuts for the wealthy while further impoverishing the rest. They don't think about the impact cutting access to health care will have on the average American. They are so focused on the next election they have to win that they don't ask, *is the Strict Father belief true? Where is the evidence for it? Can their entitlement be defended as something that's only natural? Is it really every man for himself or would some other orientation be better? Is the greed of a few really justifiable? Should we keep catering to it? How do we want to be remembered? What do we really care about?*

These are important questions that are never asked and never answered because of a single-minded pursuit of a win—a need to *get more*. We should insist that our leaders be more thoughtful—we want and need reflection and analysis from them. How can they make good decisions otherwise?

The way you were

In my abuser counseling groups, I used to try to get people to reflect on their behaviors by asking them how they would like to be remembered after they're gone, hoping that would prompt them to think about change. *What would you like to see on your headstone*, I'd ask. Many would be taken aback by the question and lots found it difficult to answer, so I'd provide a few examples.

Would you prefer that it read, I would say, "He was always right?" That's a big one. Or how about "He sure knew how to scare people?" Would that one work for you? What about this one—"He was a winner!" Maybe you would like it to say, "He controlled his family well." It makes it sort of clear where many have placed their life emphasis. And when they have an opportunity to reflect, it doesn't sound too good. Being right, winning, trying to never be weak, and using fear and other tactics to maintain control aren't exactly headstone material, are they?

Likewise, how would our unusual suspects like to be remembered? Would they prefer "He took health care and infant formula and food away from single mothers and children and gave the savings to the very wealthy"? How does that sound? Or how about "He was in the bag for a couple of billionaires who don't care about the climate and just want to keep making money on fossil fuels"? How about this one, "He would have done anything to keep his political position, even if he sold everyone out in the process"? Or, "He just did what he had to do to survive." That's a noble one. What about this one, "He could always get away with abusing and assaulting women and treating them disrespectfully"? Got to love that one, right? We could think of lots more.

Many people, particularly younger people, will never have heard the name Lee Atwater. Lee Atwater was a political strategist in the 1980's, a primary architect behind the use of code words and ideas to make white people scared of black people, among other things. He sowed fear and divisions between people that lasted a long time—in fact, they arguably never went away—in order to win a Presidential campaign for George H. W. Bush in 1988. I mention him because as he was dying of a brain tumor, he said that he regretted what he did. His zeal to win, no matter who got hurt—his 'ends justify the means' approach—got in the way of his being decent. And he wished he could take it back.[62] If he had thought about his epitaph a lot earlier, like the abusers in my groups were asked to do, maybe things for everyone would have been a lot better. Reflection is a part of the cure for what ailed him, and other abusive personalities like him.

Politics seems like a profession that precludes reflection altogether. The focus on short-term wins and gains doesn't leave any room for it. Tweets and social media don't make it any easier. When I was growing up, there was a little poster that my dad hung in our garage. It said, "There is no expedient to which a man will not resort to avoid the real labor of thinking." Yes, thinking is *hard*. We recall that some research shows us that black and white thinking may be a trait of people who hold an abusive worldview. Maybe if they could see shades of grey, that worldview would seem a lot less sensible.

Time to choose

Neanderthal and our other unenlightened ancestors undoubtedly did things of which most of us would never approve today. Yet, it is common knowledge that some of their more unsavory characteristics and inclinations remain with us. It may be that we are genetically hardwired toward greedy, resource-grabbing aggression. Our reptilian brain is designed to live in the jungle as predator or prey and to be vigilant and ruthless. We are tribal, too, and we look upon those not like us with suspicion and hate. Our ancestors acted, out of necessity like brutes.

Natural is not inevitable

That violence has not been reduced; that war continues unabated. That we shoot each other in cars and bars and everyplace else and that people are being exposed to abuse and violence even in the supposed safety of their homes may be evidence enough of our inclinations. And all of these things have been happening since the beginning. So, when abusers make the claim that abusive behavior, aggression and violence are only natural, they could be right. But just because something is *natural*, doesn't mean that it is inevitable. There are plenty of behaviors that were once natural that clearly aren't anymore. Nobody looks to the Stone Age for advice. Nobody ever seriously asks, *what would Neanderthal do?* No, natural doesn't mean inevitable. We are capable of change. We can choose something else.

Although the concept of choice has been discussed elsewhere in this book already, it's so important that it bears repeating. Abusive behavior doesn't just happen by accident, as the abuser wants us to believe. Choices about how to behave are always being made. Who is making them and to whose benefit are the only salient questions.

Through our discussion of tactics, beliefs and motives, we have seen that what the abuser most wants is total control. He seeks to create an environment of unaccountability so that he doesn't have to answer for his actions. The abuser's partner didn't, we can surmise, just fly out the door. He didn't accidentally or unknowingly push her down the stairs. It was a choice on the part of the abuser to act the way he did. Regardless of what they want us to believe—and what they may believe themselves—abusers choose their actions.

The political leadership claims lack of choice in the same way and for the same reasons. One way in which this lack of choice is most often manifested at the level of politics is in discussions about the economy and around who gets what and why. We discussed that as a tactic in Chapter 2. For example, when some people get a lot and others get very little, we are often told that it's just the way the economy works. It's only natural. The economy has a mind of its own and we can't really control it. Therefore, it should be left alone. We accept that frame—that belief—as the truth. And that allows our suspects to keep getting away with taking all of the resources for themselves and depriving everybody else.

People who work with abusers spend much of their time highlighting the issue of choice because without it as a guiding principle, nothing will ever be different—how can it be? After all, if he didn't choose his behavior, he can't very well choose something else. If we are going to provide pressure and motivation for change, it won't work if bad actors argue successfully that they had no choice or couldn't help the bad things that happened to people because of their actions.

Pointing out, continuously, that they always have a choice in what they do is necessary for accountability in all abusers, regardless of where we find them. Though it might benefit the leadership to claim that something was out of their hands, that something had to be done, or that they couldn't help it, the reality is that they *are* choosing and that what happens to the economy and to social services and to our wellbeing *is* in their control. No amount of denial or outright lying changes that.

So, now knowing that there is hope—that there is a chance that our suspects can actually change—what are we to do? We know what needs to happen for abusive people to change, but how can we, as average people with little political power, hold our leaders accountable? How can we take action to stop our political leaders—the unusual suspects—from getting away with their abusive behavior? How can we push them toward reflection on their power and the decisions they make? What can we do to stop this trend from escalating before it's too late?

Pete's reflection

Remember the story of Pete—the man whose mother had been shaped by his father?

Through reflection, Pete has come to understand what it must be like to be on the receiving end of abuse—to have no power and few freedoms, to be servile, and to have been shaped. He gets that such an abbreviated life can't be fulfilling.

He now says this:

> What my father did to my mother is the worst thing anyone can do to a person. She was like dead. Not even human. She just served my father. She had no life or meaning. She had a house and food to eat, but she was dead.

In his mind, his mother led a wasted life—the ultimate tragedy. He can see the consequences and he doesn't want them for his family. Today, he doesn't want to cause such a condition, nor does he want to suffer it himself. Unfortunately, Pete, in taking after his father, shaped his wife so well that he now cannot undo it. He no longer wants that kind of life; he does not want that kind of partner, but he worries that it's too late. He did his work too well.

Requirements for change

Although they've been stated previously in these pages, the requirements for an abuser to reform are of such importance that it's prudent to state them once again. They are:

- Negative consequences for abusive behaviors, not rewards and applause.

- Honest self-reflection, not denial and justification.

- Acceptance that abusive behavior is always a choice, regardless of the justifications manufactured to make it appear otherwise.

It is only when these three factors are present that an abuser might reduce or eliminate his violence.

Chapter 7

The Way Out

...how deep-seated is the fear of passing judgment, of naming names and of fixing blame—especially, alas, upon people in power and high position.

—Hannah Arendt

In the last chapter, we reviewed the three requirements for change: Consequences, reflection and choice. We *must* experience consequences for our actions if we are going to decide to change any of them. Then, we reflect on those consequences—those that affect us and those that affect others. Were they positive or not? Finally, we accept that no matter how we might think or even wish otherwise, we are in control of our actions. Abusive behavior might be natural, but it isn't inevitable. We can decide what to do and who to be. We have a choice. And then we change—or don't.

We often say that domestic violence causes an awful set of consequences, but here is the thing: Domestic violence doesn't cause anything—the domestic abuser does. It's not abuse that's the problem; it's abusers. If we want to attach responsibility to those who deserve it, we have to address them directly. The way we speak matters; it frames the problem. To effect change, we will have to get specific and personal.

Naming names

When "domestic violence" is the problem, there is nothing we can do to change it—that is simply what domestic violence is. But when we can change our language and place the actual abuser at the center of the violence, things look different. If any person caused even one of these effects on our list of consequences, let alone many of them, we would be mortified. We would want to stop that person immediately from ruining our families, our progeny and entire communities.

Placing the abuser at the center of the problem doesn't mean that we don't have sympathy or compassion for abusive people or that we cannot provide an opportunity for them to change. We understand that they engage in and carry forward the worldview that surrounds them, but we can't excuse them or allow their actions to be diluted on the grounds that they are common because, in the words of philosopher Hannah Arendt, "Where all are guilty, however, no one is."[63]

In recent years, as women and other minority groups gained more power and status, a counter response emerged, known commonly as backlash. Backlash simply means that some people want us to change back. It is an attempt to correct what some see as an unwelcome shift in the power balance.

The problem with the term is that it doesn't really mean much to most people; it has no agency. In other words, backlash isn't a person. It's a phenomenon—it doesn't do anything, so how could we ever get it to stop? Likewise, as a profession, domestic abuse counselors blame patriarchy for domestic violence, child abuse and lots of other serious problems. But patriarchy isn't a person, either—it's an idea and we can't hold an idea to account. But we *can* hold accountable those who exemplify or express the idea and carry it forth.

It doesn't help to place blame, real or rhetorical, on non-entities. So, what can we do to stop the abusive worldview or patriarchy or backlash from gaining more traction? Can we convince them to straighten up? Actual people do things and we should make that abundantly clear.

In fact, the actions of a relative few are causing our society untold grief and cost; their entitled, unaccountable behaviors make life hard for the many and we do ourselves no favor by allowing them to depersonalize the whole thing. When we fail to assign credit and blame to real people who take real actions and cause real harm, no one is accountable and bad things just keep happening with never an end in sight.

Yes, there is an abusive culture, as we have described extensively, but there are people—specific people—that participate in it and carry it forward. And they deserve to be recognized.

The election of Donald Trump is a case in point. We needed an actual person who represents this abusive mentality in order to mobilize, engage and invigorate people in opposition to it. The millions of women and men marching the day after Trump's inauguration suggests that we have found an especially good one. Hard as it is to accept Trump's unlikely ascendency, there is a silver lining. As the perfect symbol of the abusive worldview, he embodies all of it in very visible ways. He is the true, unfiltered personification of abusive leadership and because we can see it so clearly, he provides a convenient focus around which we can organize our resistance.

Of course, when he is gone—as he will be—there will be others who are perhaps worse, even more sophisticated, who will try to impose the same abusive worldview on us. But we will have been there before. We will recognize the signs even when they are subtle and we'll be better equipped to resist. By placing pressure on individual legislators and exposing them and their actions and naming names and affecting their positions, we are exercising our best hope. Obama used to say, "Make me do something." Exactly.

In the end, we should offer motivation, which can be internal or external. Sometimes change comes about because someone saw the light and wanted more and sometimes change occurs because they saw the writing on the wall from behind their crumbling gates. Sometimes they want to change. Sometimes they are compelled. Either way, it's change.

If the world isn't a competitive jungle, then what is it? If a family and a country cannot best be operated according to the rules of the Strict Father or according to the self-interest and entitlement of just a few, then how can they best be run?

We know that when all that people are doing is trying to survive, nothing productive happens. There is no progress in the jungle, save for an occasional reorganizing of the food chain. The jungle does not make for a healthy, happy society. A free-for-all where only the strong survive and where we all fight over limited resources is unsafe, unwise and ultimately unwanted. We don't want that life for people. The jungle is no great place to be, but what would be better and how do we get there? That brings us to the final question: What is the alternative worldview that we wish to put forth? We can say well enough what we don't want; we do that all the time, but what do we *want*? And how can we best describe and communicate it? Is there a way out?

I have argued that the concept of domestic violence fits what we are seeing on the national level perfectly, in both actual and metaphorical ways. There are abusers and abuser-like ideas. We can call that concept forth in order to tell the story of larger-scale abuse and the blatant misuse of power by a few. Some of our leaders behave abusively, using tactics designed to maintain their power and lessen ours. They, like their counterparts, get away with it over and over, and if they aren't stopped, they will cause our collective home to fall apart in the same way that an abuser presides over the inevitable collapse of his.

We began this book with a recognition that our messages of non-violence, peace, and compassion are not as interesting nor as motivating as those messages of winning and being right and getting all of the power and resources for oneself. Breaking through the *how to get more* message has been difficult.

Nonetheless, here is a partial list of our favorite words and ideas to get us started in thinking about the alternative:

- Cooperation
- Compromise
- Nurturance
- Partnership
- Inclusion and diversity
- Taking care of people
- Empathy
- Responsible use of power
- Actual opportunity (not rhetorical opportunity)
- Equality and a balance of power
- Peace
- Honesty and transparency—telling it like it is
- Compassion
- Choice

We want a world in which people are cared for and have some safety and security and are not treated badly or unfairly on the basis of their race or religion or gender. We want a world without bullies who hurt other people just for fun. We want justice and opportunity and resources for everybody and not just a few. That all sounds great, doesn't it? And it is! Who could disagree? Well, to those with an abusive mentality, these alternatives sound like weakness, inefficacy, powerlessness and lack of control. They don't appeal because they seem to call for giving up winning and power in favor of losing and powerlessness. Abusers hear those ideas as a mandate to be less, not more.

Many of our fellow Americans voted for a person with whom they could identify—someone after whom they wanted to model their own lives. They want to be winners. They want to be right. They want our leaders to be more powerful than other leaders. By contrast, equality, fairness and empathy sound weak and wrong-headed. Cooperation doesn't fit within the worldview of power, dominance and competition. As for empathy, those with the abusive mentality see it as something for people with less power to deal with. Powerful people, they think, don't need to understand; they need to be understood—a big difference.

The few have modeled for the many a world that is exploitative, harsh, self-centered and irresponsible. For example, former ExxonMobil CEO and current Secretary of State, Rex Tillerson, when asked his philosophy of life, responded, "Making money."[64] And naturally, making money works in tandem with getting and holding onto power. This is the model that they teach to others.

Their story promotes selfishness and greed unapologetically because the superiority of the few over the many is believed to be natural. In fact, they tell us that they are acting correctly and morally when they grab resources and power for themselves and fail to take care of people or live up to their promises. By holding onto Strict Father morality, they reassure themselves that they are teaching hard but necessary lessons to people, even when those people wind up poor, homeless or destitute.

And for some, the jungle is a perfectly apt metaphor for the kind of world that they seem to be advertising, even designing. We can imagine it. The concept of stalking, predator versus prey amorality, natural selection (survival of the fittest), and hierarchy are all on display. It's every man for himself. At the same time, as they live out and impose a harsh, every-man-for-himself, Strict Father story, they have also learned to speak in ways that disguise it.

By speaking passively—"mistakes were made"—the bad things they do begin to look like accidents. They didn't *do* anything wrong; something bad just happened naturally. The domestic abuser's wife just flew out the door. The rich just miraculously get richer. How did that happen? We have no idea. The plot in this story always includes a prescription for how they get away with it all in the end. They spin their lack of accountability and avoidance of consequences into something called "winning" and "being right." Their entitlement, institutional and otherwise, makes it difficult to confront them because their version of *how things are* seems to carry a lot of weight.

The abusive worldview and its consequences

Some people denigrate hope. They don't see it as motivating, at least not in politics. They believe, perhaps correctly, that fear reigns in politics. When fear and power are aligned, hope has no place; it's the odd man out, they seem to think. But before we give up, assuming that the story of winning and power and money—*the dark side*—will always win, we can think about how to reframe or recast their messages. But awareness and reflection are first, so let's review the main points and messages about the abusive worldview and those who carry it:

+ There is large-scale misuse of power that looks like what we see in domestic abusers. Seeking and rationalizing self-centered control and dominance is the province of the domestic abuser, but those concepts are personified more widely and ominously in abusive leadership today. We need only look at what happens in abusive homes to see what will happen to us.

+ Abuse produces consequences in our homes and on a global scale in similar ways. Helplessness, hopelessness, impoverishment, lost opportunity, reduced freedom and, ultimately, failure are likely in places where an abusive mindset is allowed to reign.

+ Families in which abuse is not stopped almost always collapse under the weight of it. They are a microcosm of what happens when inequality, disparagement and the erosion of people's freedoms operate in tandem. They are, therefore, instructive.

- Inequality leads to bad outcomes and eventual atrophy, if not widespread collapse. When a few benefit at the expense of the many, society becomes unstable. The insulated few make bad decisions that affect people negatively, even themselves. Crime, including violent crime and even murder, rises. Altruism and trust disappear. The jungle, where it's every man for himself and everyone is out to make a buck, grab resources and *get more*, prevails, but it's miserable and unsafe for everyone in the long run.

- The Strict Father approach to running a family— or a much larger enterprise—doesn't work. Loads of research backs up that claim. Allowing others to suffer and be insecure doesn't make them strong, but weak. It creates people who are fearful and aggressive. Creating a place where everyone can be safe will increase hope, creativity, productivity, happiness and wellbeing.

- Some of our leaders are not much different than those we call deadbeats. They don't meet their obligations and make excuses for their selfishness and indifference.

- Experiencing the consequences of one's behaviors is a necessary precursor to change. When our abusive leadership can hide behind gates—real and metaphorical—we won't see change. We should incite consequences—peaceful ones—whenever and wherever we can.

• Abusive beliefs and behaviors aren't "only natural." Abusers just want to convince us that the bad things that happen to us at their hands couldn't be helped, but everything is a *choice*. People *choose* to do things. Abusers *choose* to abuse. Abusive policy makers *choose* their policies. That's the language we should be using.

• If anything is going to change, we have to change our models. If our models illustrate selfishness, fear and an unquestioned desire to dominate, that is what will be imitated. If our models demonstrate a different kind of power—one based on respect and integrity and the recognition that we should all share in the largess of our families and our society—then that is what people will emulate. The code is not hard to decipher. Make our models the right ones.

• Power, in the way that it is practiced and sought by abusers, can never really be attained. If we are going to reach the adherents to and proponents of the abusive worldview, we have to reframe and turn the concepts central to abusive worldviews on their heads. We have to talk about respect, power and leadership in ways that preclude control, dominance, abuse and authoritarianism and include personal power, responsibility, awareness, choice, empathy, compassion, courage and strength. The traditionally masculine virtues of strength, bravery, self-reliance and independence don't need to be eliminated, but some of their current expressions ought to be. We need to reframe masculinity so that it can be attained *not* at someone else's expense. Women and minorities needn't be weak in order for some to be strong. We have to talk about empathy not as a weakness or tool to manipulate but as a strength, and cooperation not as an impediment to survival but as its requisite.

Abusive people, whether in our homes or in our hallowed halls, all rely on similar tactics and strategies, hold onto the same beliefs, and act on the same motives. They have the desire to get and keep power, and that is the central part of their abuse. But the pursuit of total power through domination is, in the end, whether political or personal, not powerful at all.

It is up to us to frame possibilities in a way that engages, appeals to, and makes sense for the people we most wish to persuade. The question is, *how can we all get more?* Therein lies the challenge. Whether we inherited some propensity for violent, abusive behavior or not, whether we are afraid or not, whether we like violence or not, whether it works well or not, whether we live in the jungle or not, we can and must choose the conditions under which we will resort to it.

Our unusual suspects, through their propaganda, control of the media, money and gerrymandering, have missed the fundamental point. Power defined and played out this way is its opposite. The longer they use these tactics and abusive behaviors, the harder we will all fall and the more power they will eventually lose. As for our culture and our country, when leadership is practiced in this way—the way that abusive men practice it in their homes—the power they wield cannot and will not last.

Pressure

Few abusers ever enter into a counseling program because they have decided that the misuse of their power is causing problems for people. Power, either the real or just for show variety, is not something that most people willingly give up. The abuser needs to experience some uncomfortable consequence if he is going to change. As our abusive political leaders secure victory after victory, despite our overwhelming disapproval, it's hard to imagine that there would be sufficient motivation for change. To the contrary, they must be thrilled and planning to stay exactly the same.

Unless and until we as a culture provide needed motivation to specific players, chances are pretty good that no change will be forthcoming. We need an outside force to supply the answer to the question, *why change?* Because most abusers won't come up with that answer on their own, that outside force will have to be us.

PAMELA JAYNE

Beyond karma

Man's capacity for justice makes democracy
possible; but man's inclination to injustice
makes democracy necessary.

—Reinhold Niebuhr

Given all that we have covered and all that we now understand about domestic abusers and their counterparts—the unusual suspects—what can we actually *do*? What kind of power do we have and how can we best use it? Granted, we know that in the end, abusers get the opposite of what they crave (whether they know it or don't) and that 'what goes around, comes around.' But while that is satisfying to know, we don't have time to wait until our abusive leadership gets around to reflecting on the futility of trying to *get more*. We must act, ourselves. Remembering our three steps to change—consequences, reflection and choice—we begin with the idea of consequences.

When authorities tell domestic abusers that their abuse is wrong and won't be tolerated, that is a consequence and an effective one. Whether any particular person changes his beliefs as a result or just realizes that there will be a price to pay for continued abusive behaviors, those kinds of messages do matter—they *do* reduce violence. Unfortunately, they aren't often offered. That is an area where we can—by working with the court system charged with holding people who do bad things to account—make some change. Sending a message of disapproval doesn't cost much and it begins to eat away at the prevailing idea held by purveyors of the abusive worldview that *abuse pays*. Of course, when an abuser's family falls apart and he loses everything, that, too, is a consequence—one that he really feels.

Consequences for continuing on an abusive path are beginning to materialize for some of these unusual suspects, too. They seem to have figured out that we know what they are up to and we aren't going to stand for it. Losing an election or fearing that they might is an obvious consequence and more than a few of our political leaders seem legitimately worried about it. Hundreds of people lining up in front of their offices and making thousands of calls may, they fear, portend the worst for them. What if having the support and financial backing of a few self-involved billionaires isn't enough to save them?

Of course, calling out their behavior and naming names, exposing what they prefer to keep hidden is a consequence. We don't allow them to make it seem like their bad behavior is *just the way things are* and that everyone is doing it because where all are guilty, no one is. If I have convinced you of nothing else, I hope that I have shown you that consequences for bad behavior are essential for change. Otherwise, they'll just keep getting away with it.

The press—the independent press—must be encouraged. They find out the truth, which might not otherwise ever see the light of day, and they are struggling under the new "press is the enemy" line enthusiastically promoted by the Trump administration and its supporters. In antidemocratic places where dictators reign, protesters and their leaders, along with press who expose and criticize those dictators, are conveniently *done away with, one way or another.* Sometimes people just metaphorically do away with themselves by keeping quiet and never criticizing. Political leaders need support or at least the appearance of it from those they intend to lead. The necessity of public support, at least for now in the US, provides us a lot of leverage and we ought to use it at every opportunity, without fail.

In the end, it appears the political leadership is not *getting away with it* quite as easily as they thought they might. We are naming names and we are fighting back.

Now, while we are waiting for the consequences that lead to reflection, which lead to choice, and finally to change (or not), we must accept the distinct possibility that a few won't be persuadable.

For example, over the course of the last several decades, groups of men—mostly men—have been claiming that their rights have been diminished in favor of greater rights for women. Known commonly as *men's rights groups,* they often point to the Violence Against Women Act as an example, claiming that the title alone—violence against women— discriminates against them. After all, they are being abused, too. They'd like us to think that all men feel the way they do, but that's just not the case.

Many men—most men, including many of our political leaders—understand full well that violence against women in this country and around the world is a serious problem. Men's rights groups are, therefore, small, with an agenda to make sure that women don't wind up with too much power or get the upper hand. They are outliers at the fringe and we ought never allow them to say otherwise without challenge. We will prevent them from just blending in with the others and camouflaging themselves. We will expose them for the viewpoints they actually hold.

What else gets in the way?

It's only normal—not!

Part of the only natural claim includes the belief that abuse and aggression are just normal and very common. Even professionals in the field make that argument routinely. When we speak to people in our communities, we often use statistics to show that domestic violence affects a whole bunch of people. We want our communities to recognize the scope and gravity of the problem, which is understandable, but what are the effects of such statements?

When we claim that everybody is doing something, or that some behavior is just normal and very common, we excuse it and inadvertently make it okay for lots more people to do it with impunity. Known as social norming, we might unwittingly give abusers fewer reasons to change—and *fewer reasons* is not what they need.

Speeding is illegal, but everyone does it and nobody feels like a terrible person when they do. Let's face it, the main consideration when deciding to speed is whether we might get caught. But we don't want people to believe that domestic violence is like speeding, technically illegal, but otherwise just normal and widespread, because that gives everyone permission to do it all the more. In fact, perpetrating and promoting the abusive worldview is the province of a relatively small group. Most people don't agree with it and we don't want to encourage them to change their minds under peer pressure.

The Right—the unusual suspects—have been getting away with obstructionism and abuse by making it seem like everybody does it. Their problem behaviors spill over onto Progressives, and it starts to look like everybody is equally involved in creating chaos and havoc. It isn't just *them* holding up everything and gumming up the works. It isn't just Republicans. It's Democrats and Independents, too, we are told. It's the entire Congress—it's everybody—and so we can't tell who or what is actually responsible. All we know is that things are in quite a mess. Nothing can be done, we lament. Consequently, accountability never attaches to the people who deserve it. It's a deflection.

We don't want to imply that all men are abusive. We don't want to suggest that abusers are in every home. We don't want to say that all politicians and their ilk are abusive and so what difference can we make anyway? The more we talk about how common it is, the more we will excuse it, confuse people, and make it okay.

There aren't two sides, there is one. And not everything is equal. There are specific people who cause these problems.

There are specific people who sell us all out for their personal enrichment and self-aggrandizement. There are people who lie and cheat their constituents and act outrageously and selfishly under the radar. But there are also those who don't and we must be very careful not to suggest otherwise lest some people, thinking that everybody does it, decide to just get on board.

Whether any of our suspects change or don't, we can change what we do in response to them and that may get us headed in the right direction. Yes, they are tricky. Yes, they are clever. In fact, they are positively Machiavellian and in the past, we've been no match for them. But we can be every bit as clever. And we're going to need to be from this day forward.

What to do?

The work and experience of domestic violence professionals may be instructive to the whole. In fact, the trauma we have experienced as this abusive worldview and its carriers have been foisted upon us can absolutely be reduced. What we know from working with organizations that deal with trauma is that there are actions we can take to be more resilient and to remain strong for the battles ahead.

First, we connect with others. Marches around the world on the day after Trump's inauguration went a *long* way to empowering us and giving us hope. The feeling of being alone, isolated and without support allows the abuser to continue with his plans unimpeded. And that's why support groups remain a staple of what domestic violence programs offer victims. Support groups are designed to reduce feelings of isolation and to connect people to others with similar problems. We know that they work to help people recover.

Research done by Cris Sullivan of Michigan State University specifically shows us that domestic violence advocates, in connecting victims to one another, contribute significantly to the long-term wellbeing of victims and their children.[65] They give them hope—yes hope matters—and a sense of self-efficacy. They help them to realize their potential and the control that they actually can have over their own lives— control often taken from them by their association with abusers and the abusive worldview.

Next, we can demand that those who are philosophically aligned with us and who have some power and influence stand up and do what is needed. Advocates, who often have some power because of their positions, stand up for victims when various groups don't understand them or don't produce what victims need. Advocates make sure that those on the outside, like the criminal justice system, hear victims' voices even though that system might not always want to listen. And they pressure those systems to change. We need advocates like this, too, on a larger scale. We need people with *power* to do something. We can't let up on that demand. We can't do it all alone.

Of course, we all have to stand up and support the people who have been most marginalized, frightened and treated abusively because of their race, gender, religion or origin. We are all in this together. Everybody matters or nobody does.

We must also be unafraid and speak the truth about what we see. It's easy to be conned and manipulated and silenced by abusive forces, as we have seen. But the only ones to benefit from our silence is them. The time for being nice—or worse, invisible—is clearly over. That doesn't mean that we adopt the vulgarity and self-centered, adolescent behaviors that are present in our leadership today. It means that we simply say that which is true. And if our circumstances prevent us from doing so, we empower others in our place. Fortunately, there are large numbers of people who have had enough—women foremost among them. They are standing up, speaking out and adopting strategies to force change, exposing the few in order to save the many. That's our work now.

The abusive worldview is antidemocratic entirely by design. We could wait around for the abusive leadership to bestow more democracy on us or let us keep the little we have left, but that would be foolish because left to their own devices they definitely won't do it. So, we create it ourselves. From working with victims, we know that empowerment is very, very important. And it is the cure for the apathy that the abusive worldview and its carriers produce. We can do it. We *are* doing it. And we are going to keep it up.

Who should leave?

Victims are often the ones who have to leave their homes when the abuser makes it too dangerous to stay. Frankly, I think that's wrong, don't you? Why should they be the ones to move while the abuser stays at home resting in his La-Z-Boy and watching TV? Likewise, many people are planning to leave the US and the impulse is completely understandable. But why should we, the vast majority, have to leave our own country because a few abusers have taken over? They should be the ones to leave, not us and we can see to it that they do.

If those who purport to lead us can't or won't—or at least don't—do it well, and if they continue on their mission of manipulating us and trying to reduce or limit our power while bolstering theirs, we can organize and get them out. To use the title of my earlier book, we can simply *ditch those jerks*. Of course, it would be best to identify them before they gain too much power—before ditching is our only option.

Warning Signs

There is an unusually large collection of abusers in the ranks of politicians. Maybe politics attracts them or maybe it eventually corrupts them. Either way, they get to live out their abusive worldview without guilt and mostly without consequence.

People seem disbelieving of the actions of our unusual suspects in the furtherance of the abusive worldview. That kind of incredulity is similar to that expressed by people concerning the domestic abuser. He can't possibly be *that* bad, they think. But they are often wrong.

What we need is an abuse prevention program to stop the ascendancy of these abusive people in the future. Therefore, we need an assessment tool—a way to identify who fits into the abusive category. And although we have discussed the details throughout this book, we will review and highlight the most important warning signs—information that, where available, will help us steer clear of the abusive worldview and its carriers.

1. **Lies and spin.**
   Abusers lie easily and frequently when it serves their purposes. They make what is bad sound good. It's a specialty. If someone lies a lot, they cannot be trusted to use their power responsibly.

2. **Lack of conscience and absence of empathy.**
   Many abusers lack empathy for others. As many as two-thirds of them probably have narcissistic or antisocial personalities. That means that they think about their own wellbeing and no one else's.

3. **Winning and survival.**
   Theirs is a worldview where every bad behavior is justified by the need to win and survive. It's all a contest with winners and losers. Watch out for signs that anyone justifies bad behavior on the grounds that it's *just the way things are.*

4. **Entitlement and exceptionalism.**
   A sense of entitlement and being above rules that apply to others is a definite warning sign. Seeing themselves as exceptional and not subject to the rules makes them dangerous.

5. **Getting away with it.**
   Many abusers believe they can skirt by and avoid the consequences of their behavior. They are very good

at avoiding accountability by any means. People who just keep "getting away with it" will only get worse.

6. **Misogyny and racism.**
   People often ask, "Do abusers hate women?" Some do—at the very least they may view themselves as superior to them. Such beliefs reflect a larger view that some people are just plain better than others. And those 'inferior' groups should be kept in their places. The belief in one's essential superiority gives them permission to take advantage of or hurt others.

7. **Threats, intimidation and control.**
   Self-explanatory. That's what abusers do.

8. **Disparagement.**
   Blame and criticize and insult anyone and everyone who disagrees. Abusers begin with flattery and end with disparagement—they use whichever works best. Constant denigration is something abusers do well.

9. **Playing the victim.**
   They portray themselves as victims because it justifies the abusive treatment of others. People who blame others and refuse to accept responsibility are to be worried about.

10. **Double standards.**
    Abusers project onto others what they themselves plan to do. Pay close attention to what they complain about because it exposes their aims and plans precisely.

11. Acting like a savior.
They talk about saving and rescuing people a lot. That bolsters them and demoralizes everybody else.

12. Using only short-term thinking.
They think only of what works now, in the short term to win, be right and survive. They rarely, if ever, reflect on their behavior or the larger values that guide that behavior.

13. Fear.
Many feel fear, act on fear, and use fear to motivate people and control them.

14. Pretending to have no choice.
Many pretend that whatever bad thing they do just can't be helped. It had to be done. When people don't choose their bad behaviors, they can't choose something else and they, therefore, can never change.

So where should we go from here? I understand that the bulk of this book has been about outlining the problem—creating awareness—and that matters because awareness is the first step in any change. But it's only a step—and not by itself sufficient to create change. Now it's time for action, action, action!

Power talk

Domestic violence professionals, people familiar with domestic abusers—the usual suspects—have a lot to offer in a growing conversation about abusive power. We have been fighting the misuse of power for many decades and not without success. We recognize it when we see it—we understand the motivations for it, the tactics in support of it, and its consequences. We name it and call people to account. There *are* ways to fight powerful, abusive interests. And now, it's all hands on deck. We have our to-do list. First up is the task of exposing them. We must shine a light on their behaviors, underlying beliefs and the real consequences that they produce.

Next, we stop trying to please them or to give them what they want. We don't appease them because they will always want *more*. In fact, their demands will only escalate. It's true that they would prefer we just stay quiet—and they'd like to fool us into thinking that they are something that they aren't. Of course, it works best for them if we believe that there are two sides to every implausible story they tell, when in fact, there is often just one.

They hope that we agree that it's a winner take all world, where only the strong survive (them), and where exploitation and abuse are just normal and natural. They would like us to feel grateful for whatever scraps we are thrown. Therefore, we do the opposite. If something works for them, in any way, to maintain their powerful positions, we should think twice about accepting it because it very likely won't work for us. If they can divide us, they will conquer us. If they can silence us, they will beat us. But neither is inevitable.

Next, we identify our points of leverage—usually, that means affecting their positions of power—and we keep them under constant, unrelenting pressure. We never allow them to just forget about it. How do we keep reminding them? We talk. We write. We connect. We confront. We think. And of course, we vote, which, hopefully, still means something.

We ought not waste too much time on people who just aren't persuadable. Anyone who has tried to talk a close friend or relative out of an abusive relationship knows how hard that is to do. The more you try to convince them, the less likely they are to be convinced—we only produce a hardening of their support for the abuser. They believe that we just don't understand the abusive person, who is after all, in their view, a good person deep down who is really trying, or they conclude that *we* must be the bad ones after all. Trump supporters are like that—the harder we argue for our point, they harder they argue for theirs and the gulf between us just grows.

Most importantly, we don't believe the spin that comes from our unusual suspects. We don't believe their stories about us. When they disparage us, we understand that they do it in furtherance of their selfish, abusive interests. It's not about us—it's about them. We don't accept their double standards. We don't agree that we need to be made over or saved. We reveal who they truly are—stealth and hiding only works for them. We ask ourselves whether their explanations and justifications are logical and reasonable. We ask who benefits from this or that policy or action. We ask ourselves whether their vision of the world contributes to or detracts from the welfare of the whole. Finally, we focus on what they do and never on what they say. *Never.* As we know, denial and lies are a crucial element in the abuser's arena and abusers can be quite convincing. But actions? They don't lie.

Just as an abuser eventually loses power and influence with his family, we can expect that the few who occupy positions of so-called leadership will eventually suffer a similar fate, but only with a lot of help from us and our friends. It may take some time and some consistent, pressure-filled resistance, but the result is practically guaranteed.

Exposure, unrelenting pressure and unpleasant consequences are the cure for what ails our unusual suspects. Let's spread these ideas around as a strong countermeasure to abusive culture. Blogs, social media, twitter—whatever works—is what we should all do now. Let's expose it. Let's end it. Let's ditch those jerks if need be. Only we have that power—let's use it.

Although I limited the number of examples of abusive behavior—the book did need to end at some point—it would be a good idea for all of us to keep expanding the list and lending our voices. Let's continue the conversation.

Email me at pamelajayne@powerdogpress.com for more information. Stay tuned.

—Pamela Jayne

End Notes

1. Tim Snyder, *On Tyranny: Twenty Lessons from the Twentieth Century* (New York: Penguin, 2017).

2. Al Franken, *Lies: And the Lying Liars Who Tell Them* (New York: Penguin, 2003).

3. Bill O'Reilly, *The O'Reilly Factor: The Good, the Bad, and the Completely Ridiculous in American Life* (New York: Broadway Books, 2000).

4. Paul Rosenberg, "This Is Why Conservatives Win: George Lakoff Explains the Importance of Framing — And What Democrats Need to Learn," *Salon*, November 22, 2014, http://www.salon.com/2014/11/22/this_is_why_conservatives_win_george_lakoff_explains_the_importance_of_framing_and_what_democrats_need_to_learn/.

5. Anna Altman, "The Year of Hygge, the Danish Obsession with Getting Cozy," *The New Yorker*, December 18, 2016, http://www.newyorker.com/culture/culture-desk/the-year-of-hygge-the-danish-obsession-with-getting-cozy.

6. Thomas Frank, *What's the Matter with Kansas?: How Conservatives Won the Heart of America* (New York: Henry Holt and Company, 2004).

7. Pamela Jayne, *Ditch that Jerk: Dealing with Men Who Control and Abuse Women* (Alameda, CA: Hunter House, 2000).

8. Niv Elis, "Sanders, Mulvaney Clash Heatedly Over Trump Budget," *The Hill*, May 25, 2017, http://thehill.com/policy/finance/335121-sanders-mulvaney-clash-heatedly-over-trump-budget.

9. Paul Ryan, interview by George Stephanopoulos, *This Week with George Stephanopoulos*, ABC, May 7, 2017.

10. Julia Carrie Wong and Sam Levin, "Republican Candidate Charged with Assault After 'Body-Slamming' Guardian Reporter," *The Guardian*, May 25, 2017, https://www.theguardian.com/us-news/2017/may/24/greg-gianforte-bodyslams-reporter-ben-jacobs-montana.

11. Ibid.

12. David Brock, *The Republican Noise Machine: Right-Wing Media and How It Corrupts Democracy* (New York: Three Rivers Press, 2004).

13. Ibid.

14. Jacques Ellul, *Propaganda: The Formation of Men's Attitudes* (New York: Knopf, 1968). Emphasis added.

15. Matt Labash, interview by Dan Rohn, *JournalismJobs.com*, May 2003.

16. David Folkenflik, "Behind Fox News' Baseless Seth Rich Story: The Untold Tale," *NPR*, August 1, 2017, http://www.npr.org/2017/08/01/540783715/lawsuit-alleges-fox-news-and-trump-supporter-created-fake-news-story.

17. Olivia Beavers, "Congressional Exemption from GOP Healthcare Plan to Be Addressed Separately," *The Hill*, May 3, 2017, http://thehill.com/homenews/senate/331867-republicans-can-exempt-themselves-from-obamacare-rollbacks-in-new-legislation.

18. Frank, *What's the Matter with Kansas?*, 2004, 159.

19. Michael Savage, "April 20, 2017," *The Savage Nation*, Newsradio 910, York, PA, WSBA, April 20, 2017.

20. Daily Mail Reporter, "'Rush Limbaugh Said I Looked Like a Dog': Chelsea Clinton Reveals How Talk Show Host Made Fun of Her Looks When She Was Just 13 Years Old." *Daily*

Mail, April 3, 2012, http://www.dailymail.co.uk/news/
article-2124301/Chelsea-Clinton-tells-Rush-Limbaugh-fun-
looks-13-comparing-dog.html#ixzz4nPNuDMed.

21. Edward Helmore, "Trump New York Co-Chair Makes Racist
'Gorilla' Comment About Michelle Obama," *The Guardian*,
December 24, 2016, https://www.theguardian.com/us-
news/2016/dec/23/donald-trump-carl-paladino-michelle-
obama.

22. Jerry Falwell, interview by Pat Robertson, *The 700 Club with
Pat Robertson*, CBN, September 14, 2011.

23. Josh Hafner, "Donald Trump Loves the 'Poorly Educated'
— And They Love Him," *USA Today*, February 24,
2016, https://www.usatoday.com/story/news/politics/
onpolitics/2016/02/24/donald-trump-nevada-poorly-
educated/80860078/.

24. George Orwell, *Nineteen Eighty Four* (London: Martin Secker
& Warburg, 1949).

25. Elle Hunt, "Trump's Inauguration Crowd: Sean Spicer's
Claims Versus the Evidence," *The Guardian*, January 22, 2017,
https://www.theguardian.com/us-news/2017/jan/22/trump-
inauguration-crowd-sean-spicers-claims-versus-the-evidence.

26. Matthew Yglesias, "5 Times Trump Tweeted That He Would
Never Cut Medicaid," *Vox*, June 23, 2017, https://www.vox.
com/policy-and-politics/2017/6/23/15862312/trump-
medicaid-promise.

27. Orwell, *Nineteen Eighty Four*, 1949.

28. G. K. Chesterton. *The Man Who Was Thursday: A Nightmare*,
(Bristol, UK: J. W. Arrowsmith, 1908).

29. Mick Mulvaney, interview by Joe Scarborough, Mika
Brzezinski and Willie Geist, *Morning Joe*, MSNBC, March 14,
2017.

30. Ben Stein, "In Class Warfare, Guess Which Class Is Winning," *The New York Times*, November 26, 2006, http://www.nytimes.com/2006/11/26/business/yourmoney/26every.html.

31. Anat Shenker-Osorio, *Don't Buy It: Talking Nonsense About the Economy* (New York: Public Affairs, 2012).

32. Ibid.

33. Ibid.

34. Ibid.

35. Aaron T. Beck, *Prisoners of Hate: The Cognitive Basis of Anger, Hostility, and Violence* (New York: Harper Collins, 1999).

36. Rollo May, *Power and Innocence: A Search for the Sources of Violence* (New York: Norton, 1972).

37. John T. Jost et al. "Political Conservatism as Motivated Social Cognition," *Psychological Bulletin* 129, no. 3 (2003): 339-75.

38. Ibid.

39. Chris Deaton, "Protester Would Be 'Carried out on a Stretcher' in the Old Days, Trump Reminisces," *The Weekly Standard*, February 23, 2016, http://www.weeklystandard.com/protester-would-be-carried-out-on-a-stretcher-in-the-old-days-trump-reminisces/article/2001211.

40. Sam Seder, GOP Tea Party to Uninsured: Yeah, DIE!, podcast audio, *The Majority Report*, YouTube, September 13, 2011, https://www.youtube.com/watch?v=jevl2dY8oRI.

41. George Lakoff, *Moral Politics: How Liberals and Conservatives Think* (Chicago: University of Chicago Press, 1996).

42. Ibid.

43. Ibid.

44. Stephen J. Ducat, *The Wimp Factor: Gender Gaps, Holy Wars, and the Politics of Anxious Masculinity* (Boston: Beacon Press, 2005).

45. Vincent J. Felitti et al., "Relationship of Childhood Abuse and Household Dysfunction to Many of the Leading Causes of Death in Adults," *American Journal of Preventive Medicine* 14, no. 4 (1998): 245-58.

46. Esther Entin, "How Family Violence Changes the Way Children's Brains Function," *The Atlantic*, January 2, 2012, https://www.theatlantic.com/health/archive/2012/01/how-family-violence-changes-the-way-childrens-brains-function/250571/. Other studies have found found similar effects.

47. Erika Hayasaki, "How Poverty Affects the Brain," *Newsweek*, August 25, 2016, http://www.newsweek.com/2016/09/02/how-poverty-affects-brains-493239.html.

48. Richard Wilkinson and Kate Pickett, *The Spirit Level: Why Equality is Better for Everyone* (New York: Penguin, 2010).

49. Frederic L. Pryor, "The Impact of Income Inequality on Values and Attitudes," *Journal of Socio-Economics* 41, no. 5. (2012): 615-22.

50. David Brady and Kevin T Leicht, "Party to Inequality: Right Party Power and Income Inequality in Affluent Western Democracies," *Research in Social Stratification and Mobility* 26 (2008): 77 - 106. doi:10.1016/j.rssm.2007.01.001.

51. Naoki Kondo et al, "Income Inequality, Mortality and Self Rated Health: Meta-analysis of Multilevel Studies," *BMJ* 339, b. 4471 (2009). doi:10.1136/bmj.b4471.

52. Rick Scott, "Orlando Shooting is an Act of Terror in Florida" (public statement, Tallahassee, FL, June 12, 2016).

53. Pryor, "The Impact of Income Inequality," 2012.

54. Frederick Solt, "Economic Inequality and Democratic Political Engagement," *American Journal of Political Science* 52, no. 1 (2008): 48-60.

55. Morgan Kelly, "Inequality and Crime," *Review of Economics and Statistics* 82, no. 4 (2000): 530-9.

56. Margot Sanger-Katz, "Income Inequality: It's Also Bad for Your Health," *The New York Times*, March 30, 2015, https://www.nytimes.com/2015/03/31/upshot/income-inequality-its-also-bad-for-your-health.html.

57. Editorial Board, "Tom Price's Dubious Trades in Health Care Stocks," *The New York Times*, January 18, 2017, https://www.nytimes.com/2017/01/18/opinion/tom-prices-dubious-trades-in-health-care-stocks.html.

58. J. Carlisle Larsen, "Wisconsin-based Center for Media and Democracy Sues for Pruitt's Emails," *Wisconsin Public Radio*, February 17, 2017, https://www.wpr.org/wisconsin-based-center-media-and-democracy-sues-pruitts-emails.

59. Aaron Blake, "Tillerson Says Trump 'Pressed' Putin on Russia's Hacking. But It Doesn't Sound Like He Pressed Very Hard," *Washington Post*, July 7, 2017, https://www.washingtonpost.com/news/the-fix/wp/2017/07/07/tillerson-says-trump-pressed-putin-on-russian-hacking-but-the-evidence-suggests-not-so-much/?utm_term=.8f6eda8e3173.

60. Adam Schiff, "Schiff: Putin Aims to Take Down Liberal Democracy. To Put America First, Trump Must Stand Up to Him," *The Daily Beast*, July 6, 2017, http://www.thedailybeast.com/schiff-putin-aims-to-take-down-liberal-democracy-to-put-america-first-trump-must-stand-up-to-him.

61. Jared Diamond, *Collapse: How Societies Choose to Fail or Survive* (New York: Penguin Books, 2005).

62. "Gravely Ill, Atwater Offers Apology," *The New York Times,* January 13, 1991, http://www.nytimes.com/1991/01/13/us/gravely-ill-atwater-offers-apology.html.

63. Hannah Arendt, "A Special Supplement: Reflections on Violence," *The New York Review of Books,* February 27, 1969.

64. Rex Tillerson, interview by Charlie Rose, *CBS News,* CBS, March 2013.

65. Cris M. Sullivan, "The Impact of Domestic Abuse Victim Services on Survivors' Safety and Wellbeing: Research Findings to Date" (research findings, Michigan State University, n.d.), https://www.michigan.gov/documents/mdch/DomesticAbuseVictimServices_397300_7.pdf.

Bibliography

Altman, Anna. "The Year of Hygge, the Danish Obsession with Getting Cozy." *The New Yorker*, December 18, 2016. http://www.newyorker.com/culture/culture-desk/the-year-of-hygge-the-danish-obsession-with-getting-cozy.

Arendt, Hannah. "A Special Supplement: Reflections on Violence." *The New York Review of Books*, February 27, 1969.

Beavers, Olivia. "Congressional Exemption from GOP Healthcare Plan to Be Addressed Separately." *The Hill*, May 3, 2017. http://thehill.com/homenews/senate/331867-republicans-can-exempt-themselves-from-obamacare-rollbacks-in-new-legislation.

Beck, Aaron T. *Prisoners of Hate: The Cognitive Basis of Anger, Hostility, and Violence*. New York: Harper Collins, 1999.

Blake, Aaron. "Tillerson Says Trump 'Pressed' Putin on Russia's Hacking. But It Doesn't Sound Like He Pressed Very Hard." *Washington Post*, July 7, 2017. https://www.washingtonpost.com/news/the-fix/wp/2017/07/07/tillerson-says-trump-pressed-putin-on-russian-hacking-but-the-evidence-suggests-not-so-much/?utm_term=.8f6eda8e3173.

Brady, David and Kevin T Leicht. "Party to Inequality: Right Party Power and Income Inequality in Affluent Western Democracies." *Research in Social Stratification and Mobility* 26 (2008): 77-106. doi:10.1016/j.rssm.2007.01.001.

Brock, David. *The Republican Noise Machine: Right-Wing Media and How It Corrupts Democracy*. New York: Three Rivers Press, 2004.

Chesterton, G. K. *The Man Who Was Thursday: A Nightmare*. Bristol, UK: J. W. Arrowsmith, 1908.

Daily Mail Reporter, "'Rush Limbaugh Said I Looked Like a Dog': Chelsea Clinton Reveals How Talk Show Host Made Fun of Her Looks When She Was Just 13 Years Old." *Daily Mail*, April 3, 2012. http://www.dailymail.co.uk/news/article-2124301/Chelsea-Clinton-tells-Rush-Limbaugh-fun-looks-13-comparing-dog.html#ixzz4nPNuDMed.

Deaton, Chris. "Protester Would Be 'Carried out on a Stretcher' in the Old Days, Trump Reminisces." *The Weekly Standard*, February 23, 2016. http://www.weeklystandard.com/protester-would-be-carried-out-on-a-stretcher-in-the-old-days-trump-reminisces/article/2001211.

Diamond, Jared. *Collapse: How Societies Choose to Fail or Survive*. New York: Penguin Books, 2005.

Ducat, Stephen J. *The Wimp Factor: Gender Gaps, Holy Wars, and the Politics of Anxious Masculinity*. Boston: Beacon Press, 2005.

Editorial Board. "Tom Price's Dubious Trades in Health Care Stocks." *The New York Times*, January 18, 2017. https://www.nytimes.com/2017/01/18/opinion/tom-prices-dubious-trades-in-health-care-stocks.html.

Elis, Niv. "Sanders, Mulvaney Clash Heatedly Over Trump Budget." *The Hill*, May 25, 2017. http://thehill.com/policy/finance/335121-sanders-mulvaney-clash-heatedly-over-trump-budget.

Ellul, Jacques. *Propaganda: The Formation of Men's Attitudes*. New York: Knopf, 1968.

Entin, Esther. "How Family Violence Changes the Way Children's Brains Function." *The Atlantic*, January 2, 2012. https://www.theatlantic.com/health/archive/2012/01/how-family-violence-changes-the-way-childrens-brains-function/250571/.

Falwell, Jerry. *The 700 Club with Pat Robertson.* By Pat Robertson. CBN, September 14, 2011.

Felitti, Vincent J., Robert F. Anda, Dale Nordenberg, David F. Williamson, Alison M. Spitz, Valerie Edwards, Mary P. Koss and James S. Marks. "Relationship of Childhood Abuse and Household Dysfunction to Many of the Leading Causes of Death in Adults." *American Journal of Preventive Medicine* 14, no. 4 (1998): 245-58.

Folkenflik, David. "Behind Fox News' Baseless Seth Rich Story: The Untold Tale." *NPR*, August 1, 2017. http://www.npr.org/2017/08/01/540783715/lawsuit-alleges-fox-news-and-trump-supporter-created-fake-news-story.

Frank, Thomas. *What's the Matter with Kansas?: How Conservatives Won the Heart of America.* New York: Henry Holt and Company, 2004.

Franken, Al. *Lies: And the Lying Liars Who Tell Them.* New York: Penguin, 2003.

"Gravely Ill, Atwater Offers Apology." *The New York Times*, January 13, 1991. http://www.nytimes.com/1991/01/13/us/gravely-ill-atwater-offers-apology.html.

Hafner, Josh. "Donald Trump Loves the 'Poorly Educated' — And They Love Him." *USA Today*, February 24, 2016. https://www.usatoday.com/story/news/politics/onpolitics/2016/02/24/donald-trump-nevada-poorly-educated/80860078/.

Hayasaki, Erika. "How Poverty Affects the Brain." *Newsweek*, August 25, 2016. http://www.newsweek.com/2016/09/02/how-poverty-affects-brains-493239.html.

Helmore, Edward. "Trump New York Co-Chair Makes Racist 'Gorilla' Comment About Michelle Obama." *The Guardian*, December 24, 2016. https://www.theguardian.com/us-news/2016/dec/23/donald-trump-carl-paladino-michelle-obama.

Hunt, Elle. "Trump's Inauguration Crowd: Sean Spicer's Claims Versus the Evidence." *The Guardian*, January 22, 2017. https://www. theguardian.com/us-news/2017/jan/22/trump-inauguration-crowd-sean-spicers-claims-versus-the-evidence.

Jayne, Pamela. *Ditch that Jerk: Dealing with Men Who Control and Abuse Women*. Alameda, CA: Hunter House, 2000.

Jost, John T., Jack Glaser, Arie W. Kruglanski and Frank J. Sulloway. "Political Conservatism as Motivated Social Cognition." *Psychological Bulletin* 129, no. 3 (2003): 339-75.

Kelly, Morgan. "Inequality and Crime." *Review of Economics and Statistics* 82, no. 4 (2000): 530-9.

Kondo, Naoki, Grace Sembajwe, Ichiro Kawachi, Rom M. van Dam, S. V. Subramanian and Zentaro Yamagata. "Income Inequality, Mortality and Self Rated Health: Meta-analysis of Multilevel Studies." *BMJ* 339, b. 4471 (2009). doi:10.1136/bmj.b4471.

Labash, Matt. *JournalismJobs.com*. By Dan Rohn. May 2003.

Lakoff, George. *Moral Politics: How Liberals and Conservatives Think*. Chicago: University of Chicago Press, 1996.

Larsen, J. Carlisle. "Wisconsin-based Center for Media and Democracy Sues for Pruitt's Emails." *Wisconsin Public Radio*, February 17, 2017. https://www.wpr.org/wisconsin-based-center-media-and-democracy-sues-pruitts-emails.

May, Rollo. *Power and Innocence: A Search for the Sources of Violence*. New York: Norton, 1972.

Mulvaney, Mick. Morning Joe. By Joe Scarborough, Mika Brzezinski and Willie Geist. *MSNBC*, March 14, 2017.

O'Reilly, Bill. *The O'Reilly Factor: The Good, the Bad, and the Completely Ridiculous in American Life*. New York: Broadway Books, 2000.

Orwell, George. *Nineteen Eighty Four*. London: Martin Secker & Warburg, 1949.

Pryor, Frederic L. "The Impact of Income Inequality on Values and Attitudes." *Journal of Socio-Economics* 41, no. 5. (2012): 615-22.

Rosenberg, Paul. "This Is Why Conservatives Win: George Lakoff Explains the Importance of Framing — And What Democrats Need to Learn." *Salon*, November 22, 2014. http://www.salon. com/2014/11/22/this_is_why_conservatives_win_george_ lakoff_explains_the_importance_of_framing_and_what_ democrats_need_to_learn/.

Ryan, Paul. *This Week with George Stephanopoulos*. By George Stephanopoulos. ABC, May 7, 2017.

Sanger-Katz, Margot. "Income Inequality: It's Also Bad for Your Health." *The New York Times*, March 30, 2015. https://www. nytimes.com/2015/03/31/upshot/income-inequality-its-also-bad-for-your-health.html.

Savage, Michael. "April 20, 2017." *The Savage Nation*. Newsradio 910, York, PA, WSBA, April 20, 2017.

Schiff, Adam. "Schiff: Putin Aims to Take Down Liberal Democracy. To Put America First, Trump Must Stand Up to Him." *The Daily Beast*, July 6, 2017. http://www.thedailybeast.com/schiff-putin-aims-to-take-down-liberal-democracy-to-put-america-first-trump-must-stand-up-to-him.

Scott, Rick. "Orlando Shooting is an Act of Terror in Florida." Public statement, Tallahassee, FL, June 12, 2016.

Seder, Sam. *GOP Tea Party to Uninsured: Yeah, DIE!*. Podcast audio. The Majority Report. YouTube. September 13, 2011. https:// www.youtube.com/watch?v=jevl2dY8oRI.

Shenker-Osorio, Anat. *Don't Buy It: Talking Nonsense About the Economy*. New York: Public Affairs, 2012.

Snyder, Tim. *On Tyranny: Twenty Lessons from the Twentieth Century*. New York: Penguin, 2017.

Solt, Frederick. "Economic Inequality and Democratic Political Engagement." *American Journal of Political Science* 52, no. 1 (2008): 48-60.

Stein, Ben. "In Class Warfare, Guess Which Class Is Winning." *The New York Times*, November 26, 2006. http://www.nytimes. com/2006/11/26/business/yourmoney/26every.html.

Sullivan, Cris M. "The Impact of Domestic Abuse Victim Services on Survivors' Safety and Wellbeing: Research Findings to Date." Research findings, Michigan State University, n.d. https://www.michigan.gov/documents/mdch/ DomesticAbuseVictimServices_397300_7.pdf.

Tillerson, Rex. *CBS News*. By Charlie Rose. CBS. March 2013.

Wilkinson, Richard and Kate Pickett. *The Spirit Level: Why Equality is Better for Everyone*. New York: Penguin, 2010.

Wong, Julia Carrie and Sam Levin. "Republican Candidate Charged with Assault After 'Body-Slamming' Guardian Reporter." *The Guardian*, May 25, 2017. https://www.theguardian.com/us-news/2017/may/24/greg-gianforte-bodyslams-reporter-ben-jacobs-montana.

Yglesias, Matthew. "5 Times Trump Tweeted That He Would Never Cut Medicaid." *Vox*, June 23, 2017. https://www.vox.com/ policy-and-politics/2017/6/23/15862312/trump-medicaid-promise.

About the Author

Pamela Jayne is an expert in domestic violence and the author of the best-selling book on abusive men, *Ditch That Jerk*. She has been featured in numerous local and national publications such as *BBW*, *Glamour* and *Cosmopolitan* and she regularly appears on local, regional and national radio and television. She holds a bachelor's degree in psychology from the University of Michigan and a Master's degree in communication from Northern Illinois University. Jayne speaks on a variety of topics related to abuse, violence and the use of power in organizations and culture.

Made in the USA
Middletown, DE
18 August 2017